'I cannot think of any
need in childhood
as strong as the need for a
father's protection'

SIGMUND FREUD

# Dear John

# The Road to Pelindaba

*Jeff Osment*

Jeff Osment has asserted his right
under the Copyright, Designs
and Patents Act 1988 to be identified
as the author of this work

First published in Great Britain
by Lush 2018

First Edition © text
Jeff Osment

© illustrations
the artists as indicated

© photographs
the photographers as indicated

Designed by
We Are Mega Ltd

Printed in the UK
by Dayfold Ltd

ISBN 978-0-9927082-6-9
PLU 205101

A catalogue record for this book is
available from the British Library

# Contents

# Prologue

*'Dear John'* was a message in a bottle, a letter lovingly written in perfume to a long-lost father who had disappeared into Africa in 1954 when his son was still a baby, and who had never come home. That baby was Mark Constantine OBE, the perfumer and entrepreneur at the head of the global high-street brand Lush Cosmetics, and the scented message was not seeking to end a relationship but to keep it alive.

It was a story I'd heard many times, having grown up with Mark on adjacent housing estates in our home town of Weymouth in Dorset. We had met at Cub Scouts when I was ten years old, and over the next six years – through scouting, our local church and at grammar school – we began a friendship that has now spanned six decades.

For almost all of his childhood, Mark lived at his grandmother's house but, when his mother remarried in 1964, twelve-year-old Mark moved into a new home with his mother and stepfather. It was the first time he had ever had any sort of father figure in his life. His maternal grandfather had died in 1938, and Mark had never met his paternal grandfather or known much about him. Within a few months his beloved grandmother Blanche Gardner died, triggering a breakdown in Mark's relationship with his mother and particularly his stepfather. Unknown to Mark, his actual father, John Constantine, had returned to the UK from Kenya, had also remarried and was living in Gloucestershire.

I didn't know much of this at the time, except for the fact that Mark's father had joined the Royal Kenyan Police and that Mark didn't get on with his stepfather. That unhappy relationship reached a low point in the summer of 1968 when Mark failed his GCE examinations, a cardinal sin for a pupil of the grammar-school system. Unable to progress into the sixth form, unqualified for higher education or an apprenticeship, and unloved at home, the troubled teenager was running out of options.

If ever a son needed his father to provide some structure to his life, this was the time. Mark was sixteen years old, and for the previous four years his mother and stepfather hadn't spoken to him about the divorce. They had also failed to mention that Mark's paternal grandparents were still alive and living in Manchester – as they had been since the day he was born. Maybe Diane felt that she was still protecting Mark from a bad husband and father who had abandoned them when he was just a baby. Whatever her reasons, the timing was fateful.

At that very moment, forty-year-old John Constantine was preparing to leave England to start a new life in Africa. His parents would never see him again, nor would he ever make contact with his only son.

It wouldn't be long before Mark was homeless and living rough in a wood with barely a penny to his name. Yet, just seven years later, in October 1977, I drove the van when Mark delivered his first batch of handmade natural cosmetics to Anita Roddick, who had just opened her second Body Shop in Chichester. It was the beginning of a relationship that saw Mark become the major supplier of Body Shop hair and body products over the next ten years, and a leading advocate of cruelty-free cosmetics.

As an independent photographer and filmmaker, I recorded the rise of his company from a back bedroom in Mark's first house to multiple factories employing hundreds of people in Poole; I made films about henna and hair gel, lavender and rose oil; and I remember filming at the purpose-built Body Shop factory when it opened its doors in Littlehampton in December 1986 when Mark was invited to become the head of R & D at The Body Shop.

However, Mark was not one to work quietly in the background and, after ten years of close collaboration, he agreed to sell to The Body Shop the manufacturing rights to all of the products his company had invented for them. Over a three-year period The Body Shop paid Mark's company, Constantine & Weir, £9 million to take all their manufacturing in-house – not a bad return for Mark's initial outlay on a Baby Burco water boiler and some kitchen pans.

Anita and Gordon Roddick were smart enough to recognise Mark as a potential competitor and they tied him to a legally binding agreement not to open any shops on the UK high street before 1994. But at thirty-five years of age, full of energy and ambition, Mark Constantine wasn't about to retire. Instead, he retained his factories and loyal workforce in Poole and ploughed all the money into a new venture, Cosmetics To Go, a mail-order business that initially took the UK beauty world by storm.

Once again my cameras captured every episode of this extraordinary and often crazy adventure, which propelled Mark and his partners onto national television. Cosmetics To Go was the beauty version of Charlie and the Chocolate Factory. Mark was Willy Wonka and his staff were the Oompa-Loompas. The British public lapped up the wacky products on offer and the free post and packaging – a great idea if they bought dozens of products at once, but a very bad idea if they bought just one at a time. As Mark himself admitted, 'if you sell a million products and spend £1 every time you post and package them, you lose a million pounds.' In 1994 Cosmetics To Go and its parent company Constantine & Weir went into administration. Cosmetics To Go was a great business idea, but ahead of its time; the dot.com era had not yet arrived.

I've never been an employee in any of Mark's business ventures, simply a supplier of images and occasional friendly advice (which he has largely ignored). Ever since we were boys, I've been the yin to his yang: Mark impatient and impulsive, me cautious and practical; Mark the hare, Jeffrey the tortoise. No amount of advice from me could have stopped the runaway train that was Cosmetics To Go. I got off at the last station and then watched it plunge over the cliff.

Mark's innate drive to impress a father that he had never known, and his desire to find him, was pushed to the back of his mind. More years passed while Mark learned the lessons from a failed business, went back to basics, opened one small shop in Poole, and began the slow and steady rise of the global high-street brand Lush.

1988, 29 HIGH STREET POOLE

Mark photographed for the press launch of Cosmetics To Go

On the day Lush – or, as it was initially called, Cosmetic House – opened its doors in Poole High Street for the first time, there wasn't much to photograph except some black-and-white press shots of Mark and his co-founders, and it would be many years before Mark's new company required my services again.

So I too set out for pastures new, and in 1995, just as Mark was opening his first Lush shop in London, I won a filming contract with an American-owned multi-national company that would take me travelling all over the world.

Mark and I were both forty-three, and twenty-six years had passed since Mark's father had set sail and left England behind forever. It would be another seventeen years before my own journey through life and that of John Constantine would come together in a country that I was about to visit for the first time and where I would travel on the road to Pelindaba.

1994, 29 HIGH STREET POOLE

Mark with the co-founders of Lush on the opening day — Helen Ambrosen, Elizabeth Weir, Paul Greeves, Mo Constantine, and Rowena Bird with husband Mike who supported the team

# <u>01</u> Connie

A Native American medicine man called Black Elk once described life as being a trail; a path along which we travel from the moment we are born to the day of our death. On that journey we meet many people and make many decisions about our future direction of travel – decisions that have a profound impact on our lives.

In July 1969, aged sixteen, I left school as my path was leading me to art college and hopefully a career in the film industry, away from Weymouth, where I was born and raised. While the Dorset seaside resort had and still has many endearing qualities, a future in film or television wasn't one of them. This was a decision I had come to earlier in 1969 when I had applied to Bournemouth & Poole College of Art to study Photography and Film. The letter I had received after my interview, promising me a place on the condition that I achieved 5 GCE O levels in the relevant subjects, had spurred me to revise hard for my final exams.

Although the results would not be out until August, I had spent the previous two months planning my career with my best friend, Mark Constantine, while we were engaged in community work – our headmaster's punishment for pupils who eschewed sixth form and university. Mark was actually a school year ahead of me but had been kept back in the notorious form 5X, the dustbin of slackers and no-hopers. Little did anyone at the school anticipate that he would go on to become their most successful alumni ever, an inventor of cosmetics who would eventually open almost 1,000 shops in fifty countries and receive an OBE from the Queen.

At that moment in time though, Mark was interested in joining the BBC as a make-up artist, and had been advised by the county youth employment officer, that he required qualifications; either Art and History A levels or a City & Guilds Diploma in Hairdressing, which required Mark to complete a hairdressing apprenticeship. However, we were both certain of one thing as we gazed across the valley from the hillside footpath we were clearing to the hated school we were leaving: all roads led to London.

Mark had just turned seventeen and was a tall, black-haired and, I hate to say, handsome young man who never had any trouble attracting girls. Indeed, he had dedicated himself to the subject throughout his grammar-school years. 'Connie', as he was known at that time, was obsessed by girls, to the exclusion of all other school activities except English Literature and Drama. He had quickly worked out that most boys did not like Drama but many girls did, and where better to get up close and personal with girls than the school drama club? He did consider himself to be a bit of a poet and an actor, but his real ability was in the make-up department. Here he was in his element, and backstage at the school theatre was a place full of girls happy for him to apply his talent upon their hair and face.

Being a year ahead of me, Mark and I seldom mixed during school time, so I also joined the after-school drama club and bagged a leading role in a short play opposite a very confident second-year girl called Christine, one of Mark's many girlfriends. I played Algernon, a naive gentleman seeking to rescue his beloved Clara from whatever trouble she had got herself into in the Wild West, while Christine played a bar-room madam complete with bustier, stockings and garters. Looking back, it's hard to imagine a scene between a twelve-year-old boy in his uncle's top hat and tails and a thirteen-year-old girl dressed as a prostitute. Christine acted me off the stage; she was so good that when she jumped up onto the bar, hitched up her dress and flashed her legs, I didn't need to act embarrassed. That was my cue to pull her dress back down over her knees and utter the words, 'Madam, what sort of man do you take me for!' which got howls of laughter when we performed the play in front of the school.

I don't know if Mark did Christine's make-up that day, but once the make-up came off and the uniforms went back on, I barely spoke to her – or indeed to any of the other self-assured young girls who were making a big impression on a boy from a council estate. Mark, on the other hand, would walk them home three at a time.

Playing Algernon proved to be a flash in the pan, my first and last leading role, and after securing a place in the school football team, my interest in drama took second place to sport. This resulted in me seeing even less of Mark at school, as he had no interest whatsoever in sport. In fifty years, I don't think I have ever seen him run, except perhaps to chase some rare bird across a field, but that hobby didn't develop until much later.

Even at Scouts he was lazy and skived off chores. If it involved a camping knife or climbing trees, he would be at the front of the line, but when it came to washing up pans, erecting tents, or digging latrines, Mark would mysteriously disappear into the woods.

It was through scouting that we had first met. In the summer of 1963, I joined the 9th Weymouth Wolf Cub Pack, which met in a hall next to Weymouth Football Club. My mother had sent me along with a pair of pyjamas and an old lampshade for a hat, as my first Cub Scout experience was to take part in the Weymouth carnival. The theme of our float was Widow Twankey's Laundry. I put on my costume and was ushered into a chair where a boy started painting my face with a stick of make-up. He was wearing a very authentic costume with a long black plait and a 'Fu Manchu' moustache. 'What are you doing?' I asked. 'Making you look Chinese,' the young Mark Constantine replied. To this day the distinctive smell of Leichner stage make-up brings back memories of my first meeting with Mark.

I'm sure it was the smell, or is it the roar of the greasepaint, that first fired Mark's interest in make-up. But he was equally keen on creating fake wounds – particularly stage blood trickling from the corner of your mouth as you pretended to die. You could always rely on Mark to perform an agonising death scene, usually as part of a prank to fool someone that he was badly hurt. The first time you see foaming blood coming out of someone's mouth it's pretty convincing. With his tall physique, black hair and make-up skills, Mark was always a dead ringer for **Count Dracula**. Halloween couldn't come soon enough for him each year, or indeed any excuse for dressing up. His favourite look was **The Man With No Name**, aka Clint Eastwood in *A Fistful of Dollars.* Mark wore that poncho for years, along with a hand-sewn sheepskin waistcoat, which completed the look.

Despite his interest in all things theatrical, Mark always seemed to get landed with the bit parts in the school plays. A look at any school photograph and he'll be on the end of the line as a woodsman or a servant, but never the leading man. The same was true in St Edmund's Players, the church drama group that we were both involved with. I would get a small speaking part; Mark would be a guard with just a line or two at most. How did the teachers and directors of these plays not see the talent that was Mark Constantine? One theatrical producer did, however, feel the full force of Mark's fury during an audition that went spectacularly wrong.

Although as boys we watched our fair share of TV in the 1960s, some of the best comedy was on the radio, with no better example than the offbeat show of the day *I'm Sorry, I'll Read That Again* starring Tim Brooke-Taylor, John Cleese, Graeme Garden, David Hatch, Jo Kendall and Bill Oddie. It was famous for the *Angus Prune* title song and other silly songs like *Cactus in my Y-fronts* and, my personal

TOP, 1965, Weymouth Grammar School Mark far right in *The Snow Queen*
BOTTOM, 1967, Mark second from right in *Requiem for a Pharaoh*

favourite, *Identikit Gal.* Google any of these songs and you'll see why they appealed to teenage boys, as did the Prune dramas, which were spoofs of other TV and radio shows.

Mark and his classmates, Biff and Stradders, had written a spoof sketch of the current TV hit *Mission: Impossible*, which always started with the iconic title music and then a message on a tape recorder that would 'self-destruct in five seconds.' This was our comedy entry for the St Edmund's Players annual variety show 1968. Biff, who was good at science, actually made a device with wires going to some small theatrical stage whizz-bang, while Mark played Jim the secret agent who had to take on the mission. The anticipated self-destruct 'bang' turned out to be more of a smoulder, and within a short time it was clear there wasn't any laughter coming from the auditorium.

1968, ST. EDMUNDS PLAYERS Mark as a bearded guard in *The Jewels of Baghdad* standing over me begging for my life

We looked up to see that the auditioning committee had already left their seats and were drinking tea at the back of the room. Realising they didn't appreciate the satire we were performing on stage, Mark stopped our act dead in its tracks and launched a verbal tirade at the producer and his consorts, accusing them of not having the courtesy to watch our five-minute sketch, however dire they thought it was. I was shocked; no one had ever spoken to the committee like this before, with Mark announcing that he wasn't going to do any more 'fucking walk-on parts.' Instead, he walked out of the building and out of the church drama group forever.

Today, in the course of the many Lush conferences at which he speaks, Mark is most definitely the leading man, the act everyone has come to see. He strolls around the stage like he owns it, rambling from one subject to another, sometimes even reading passages from a book that has inspired or informed him. Famous for making it up as he goes along, his talks are often entertaining, while at other times they can be very deep, but as for asking him to be 'brief', forget it. There's nothing Mark likes more than being centre stage with a captive audience. Even at his daughter's wedding he gave a twenty-five-minute speech and threw in a couple of conjuring tricks for good measure!

While we were friends from an early age, we didn't truly bond until the summer of 1965 when our scout troop was invited to Camp Mohawk, a summer camp catering mainly for children of US servicemen, which was situated in a forest in Wiltshire. There was the prospect of archery, canoeing, rope-swinging, you name it. To top it off, we would meet some Native Americans of the Kiowa tribe who lived in tepees and would teach us tracking and other fieldcraft skills. It promised to be the mother of all camps, and it was: the wettest fortnight in our hitherto short lives. We were camped under trees – very bad scouting practice – so even when it wasn't raining it was constantly dripping, and neither our tents nor our clothes ever dried out. If you have ever heard the 1963 song *Hello Muddah, Hello Fadduh (A letter from Camp)* hilariously sung in a child's voice by Allan Sherman it pretty much sums up our stay at Camp Mohawk. I can still sing it word for word today, 'camp is very entertaining, and they say we'll have some fun if it stops raining... take me home oh mother, father, take me home...'

When the parents visited us at the end of the first week, half the troop went home and the remainder of us crammed into the few tents that weren't leaking or awash with mud. Mark would have gone home too if it were not for the fact that his mother and stepfather, weren't on the coach. He even tried telephoning them from the local village telephone box, but to no avail, so he was stuck with me and a handful of hardened scouts. Fortunately – just when we thought it couldn't get any wetter – the sun came out and we finally got to do some tracking and dance around the totem pole.

As an adventure-seeking young boy, the Camp Mohawk experience spurred me on to become a patrol leader and Queen's Scout, whereas Mark was gradually moving in the opposite direction. Also he had never spoken to me about the death of his beloved grandmother which I now know had a major impact on his life.

If the year following the loss of his grandmother had been a difficult one for the young Mark Constantine, by the time 1969 came around we were firm friends and the year was shaping up to be a real humdinger for both of us. Despite being made to sit through fifth form again after flunking his GCE exams the first time around, Mark realised that he was unlikely to do much better at the second attempt, and his only remaining option was the hairdressing apprenticeship.

Scouting was no longer a feature in our lives, but while Mark had given up several years back I had held on until the St Georges Day parade in April when, as Troop leader, I carried the flag and led the annual parade in the town. It should have been a high point of

Mark top, Pete and Biff in scouting anoraks

my scouting career but a group of girls from my class saw me on parade and decided to make fun of me. Sure enough, on Monday morning the blackboard in my form was adorned with a caricature of me in scouting shorts, with skinny legs and sticky-out ears. There was no two ways about it, I was going to have to stop being a good Boy Scout and become more of a Rolling Stone. I grew my hair as long as I could get away with at school, and started smoking in an attempt to foster a cool image. For me, it was now all about getting a girlfriend, and who better to get advice from than the school Lothario, my friend Mark Constantine? Lesson one: 'Girls like to date older boys.' It had never really occurred to me that the majority – if not all – of Mark's girlfriends were younger than him. Although he was in the fifth form, he should have been in the lower-sixth among the scooter-riding Mods, one of the two British youth subcultures of the 1960s. I leaned more towards the motorbike-riding Rockers, as they ruled my council estate.

As a double-fifth-former, Mark had the pick of the older fourth-form girls, the ones who were fifteen going on sixteen, whereas I had my eye on a couple of girls in my class who were sixteen going on seventeen, plus a girl in the church choir. Mark also fancied her, breaking his own rule, although technically she was two months younger than him. A pretty, raven-haired soloist, Lynda had no difficulty attracting the attention of the local boys. I suspect several of them, only got involved in church activities just to be in with a chance of dating her. That, and being paid 2/6d (25p) to sing at weddings. This was way too much competition for me – and for Mark, as it turned out. Many years later he dedicated a perfume to unrequited teenage love, although he didn't get around to telling her until she was sixty-three. Now that's what I call a crush.

The GCEs came and went, and both Mark and I felt that we had done OK. One school morning in June, a group of us was called into the hall to be informed that as we weren't continuing into the

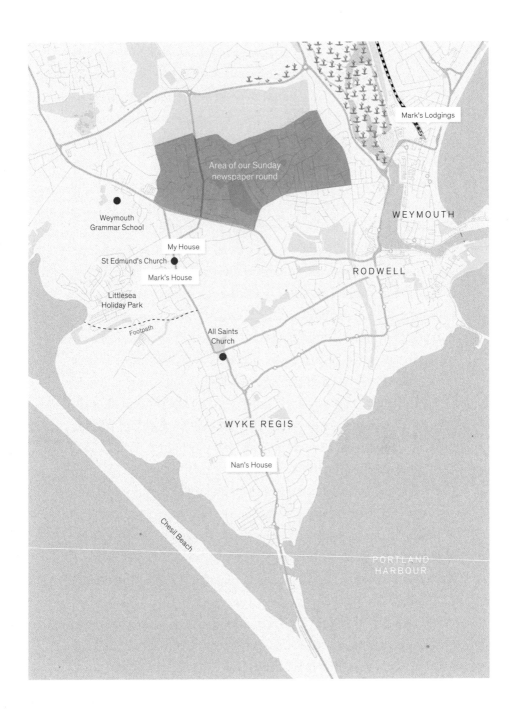

Map of the area where Mark and I grew up

sixth form we would not play any part in sixth-form acclimatisation. That was the good news. The bad news was that we were going to have to clear an overgrown footpath on behalf of the council. They actually gave us sickles and other sharp instruments with not a risk assessment in sight. The group was largely made up of 5X, of which Mark was one, a few fifth-formers like me who had chosen to go to art or technical college, and one of the most angelic girls in the school, who was on her way to motherhood aged sixteen.

The footpath in question was very close to my house, and even closer to Mark's. It linked the main road to the coastal path and when it emerged from the woods, there were panoramic views to be had over Littlesea to Chesil Beach, including the Weymouth Grammar School campus across the valley. Mark and I knew the territory like the backs of our hands. As boys we had played endless games in the woods, which contained old World War Two bunkers.

The teacher in charge of us was also leaving at the end of term. He had a very laid-back attitude to our path-clearing task and permitted us to make frequent visits to the nearby Littlesea holiday camp for drinks and ice creams. Mark and I would sit on the hill, soaking up the sun, and discuss how we would move to London at the end of our three years of further education and get a flat in the swinging capital. Once there, the BBC would not be able to refuse his hair and make-up talents, while I would be down at Pine-wood Studios, snapping clapper boards in front of Julie Andrews. I still had a fondness for her, five years after first watching *The Sound of Music.*

The girlfriend issue remained a problem and Mark advised me, once again, to aim younger, choose a sweet fourth-former and ask her out. Not for the first time, he told me about all the fourth-form girls who had dated him, which only made me feel worse. I was looking for a nice girl-next-door type to fall in love with, ideally with a name like Samantha. I was already heavily influenced by

1969, DORCHESTER

Mark and Mo with sister, Jane, and Pete

watching hours of American TV shows like *Bewitched* and saw the Hollywood lifestyle as something to aspire to.

However, just when I most needed his help, Mark seemingly disappeared off the face of the earth. When I finally caught up with him, I discovered that he had been to a beach party and got himself a new girlfriend. Not a young fourth-former, but a blossoming sixteen-year-old school-leaver from Dorchester called Mo. It took some time to get to know her, as Mark was very protective of 'little Mo' who only came up to his shoulders. Nevertheless, she must have chosen Mark with her eyes open – firstly, because she had already dated one of his mates, but also because Mark had flirted briefly with her fourteen-year-old sister, Jane. With Mark now a towering six foot in height, The Man With No Name could easily fit Mo under his poncho when it was raining. He never divulged any details about their relationship, which told me that this one was a bit special, although Mo told me many years later that she had been certain their relationship wouldn't last the summer and that she had even written Mark a letter to that effect. How wrong she was: the future Mr and Mrs Constantine OBEs had begun their journey and, for the time being, I was on my own. Bad timing as I had been counting on Mark to help me out in the girlfriend department at the upcoming end-of-year school dance.

Following Mark's advice, I had picked out a fourth-form girl I wanted to date and put her at the top of my list. I just needed to adopt some of what I saw as his 'bad boy' allure. Easier said than done. Compared to Mark's Clint Eastwood, I was the Milky Bar Kid. Nevertheless, after seeing, and even photographing, the TV pictures of Neil Armstrong setting foot on the Moon a few days earlier, I too was ready to take 'one giant leap' at the school dance. Although I spent the first hour in the nearby pub acquiring Dutch courage.

The school hall was packed and rocking with covers of all the hits of 1969 performed by a local band. I had overdone it a bit on

1970, WEYMOUTH
Geri and me, first Selfie

the vodka and lime, so I was ready to party and headed straight for a group of classmates who relished telling me that the girl in question was unwell and not at the dance. However, in their defence, they did introduce me to another girl, someone I had never seen at school before as she had only recently moved down from London. She had a pretty face, shoulder-length light-brown hair and a nice smile, so I dragged her onto the dance floor just as the band were striking up *Proud Mary*. I would never have done that sober, but she was game for a laugh. We stayed on the dance floor through *Bad Moon Rising* all the way to the last dance, *Something in the Air*, by which time I had found out her name was Geri, although it was a bit of a shock to discover that she was practically the youngest girl in the fourth form. It was even more alarming to find out that Mark had been chatting her up a few months earlier as she was on his dinner table at school.

I was happy as Larry: I'd left school, got a nice girlfriend and passed seven GCE O Levels – including French, 'quelle surprise!' I was on my way to Bournemouth & Poole College of Art and a career in the film industry. Mark, predictably, didn't get great GCE grades, and in September he started work as an apprentice hairdresser in a salon in St Albans Street, in Weymouth town centre. However we'd both achieved the first stage of our grand plan. I was about to embark on a three-year journey, which turned out to be one of the best times of my life. However, Mark still had major issues on the home front, and they were about to get a whole lot worse.

# $\underline{02}$ Nan

Over the years, I knew that Mark had made numerous attempts to find his father, even employing a private detective, and at one time phoning every John Constantine in the telephone directory. It had never occurred to him that either of his paternal grandparents might still be alive because there was so little evidence of his father's family - verbally, written down or in pictures. When a German filmmaker made a documentary of his life in 2010, Mark asked me if I had any photographs of him as a boy. Apart from one picture of Mark as a baby in his father's arms, another with his grandmother, and one of him at the 1965 Weymouth carnival, he didn't have any photographs of himself until he was a teenager. This struck me as odd, but he explained that his mother had lost them all.

My late mother, on the other hand, had kept boxes of old photographs and among them were a few of Mark and me at school or in various amateur drama productions, but nothing of him under the age of twelve. The missing pictorial history of Mark's life nagged away at me from that point onwards. As a photographer and filmmaker my job was to record events for posterity; surely, somewhere there had to be photographic evidence of Mark's early years and those of his father and grandparents?

I had dabbled in genealogy when I was younger but that was in the pre-internet days when you physically had to visit the Public Record Office in London to find documents relating to your family

1965, WEYMOUTH

A rare photograph of Mark at the
Weymouth Carnival

history. I had scanned endless rolls of microfilm, searching for my ancestors in census returns and had spent whole days reading parish records in the county record office. The census returns are only made public every 100 years, and in 2011 the 1911 census became available for viewing. This sparked a lot of online advertisements encouraging people to register with family-history websites, and so I signed up for a fourteen-day free trial with Ancestry.co.uk. I soon discovered that what would previously have taken me months could now be done in seconds. I took out a year's subscription, promising my wife that I would try to find her mother's Irish connection. After just a few evenings' research I became addicted to delving into all the records that could be accessed on the database. I still couldn't find my fourth great-grandfather but I did solve the riddle of my mother-in-law's grandmother, who wasn't Irish at all but born on the Isle of Wight.

It was gone midnight one October evening when I had the idea to trace Mark's family tree in time for his sixtieth birthday the following July. I had nine months to do it and, while I knew it was no way to find a father who had gone missing in Kenya, I felt I could at least try to discover Mark's roots. Even if I had no luck finding out what happened to his father, I knew Mark was equally keen to learn more about his maternal grandparents, Fred and Blanche Gardner, and the grocer's shop they kept in Dorchester before the Second World War.

All family histories begin with anecdotal evidence, so I started with the few facts that I knew to be true. Mark was born in 1952, the year Queen Elizabeth II succeeded to the throne. He beat me into the world by five months, arriving in Kingston Surrey on 21st July.

Mark had told me that his father, John Constantine, married his mother, Diane Gardner, in 1950 in her home parish of All Saints, Wyke Regis in Weymouth. John had been serving in the RAF when they met in 1948, which took him briefly to Rhodesia (now Zimbabwe) as well as to a post-war radar outpost on the Dorset coast near Weymouth. However, by 1950 he was a twenty-two-year-old police constable serving in the London Met.

Perhaps his short African experience sowed a seed for foreign adventure as, within eighteen months of fatherhood, John Constantine was applying to join the Royal Kenyan Police. At that time there was a rebellion, known as the Mau Mau Uprising, in the then-British colony of Kenya, and police officers in the UK were being sought to reinforce and lead the local police in communities across the country. On offer were a significant salary increase and the starting rank of Assistant Inspector. It was hardly the place to take a young wife and a barely year-old baby, but John decided to leave for Kenya and send for his wife

1949, WYKE REGIS, WEYMOUTH

Mark's father John Constantine in RAF uniform with Diane Gardner and child once he had settled in and found a home.

Years later, Diane admitted to Mark that she had never had any intention of following John to Kenya. She had already discovered that her husband was a bit of a philanderer and a gambler, and he had left her with debts, which were paid off by his colleagues in the police force. They also provided the train fare for her and baby Mark to return home to her mother in Wyke Regis, and wait to see if John's departure was a moment of madness or the long goodbye. It turned out to be the latter, and so Mark never got to know his father and spent the first ten years of his life being raised by his grandmother while his mother worked at the local newspaper office.

Although I never met Mark's grandmother, Blanche Gardner was by all accounts quite a woman. I couldn't find her on the 1911 census, but she was registered on the 1901 census as eight-year-old Blanche Rudkins living with her family in East Ham, London. I soon discovered that she came from a long line of London dock workers,

1911, MANHATTAN, NYC
Mark's grandparents Fred and Blanche Gardner Wedding Portrait

but I couldn't find any marriage to a Fred Gardner, only the birth of a son, Frederick Arthur Gardner in October 1911.

Mark had told me that his maternal grandfather had gone to New York to learn about food refrigeration before the First World War, and he had a portrait photograph of Fred and Blanche taken around that time. It took months of searching ships' passenger lists on the ancestry website, but eventually I discovered Fred and Blanche travelling as husband and wife on a ship from Liverpool to Philadelphia in 1909.

Blanche had eloped with Fred at the age of eighteen, and after an online search of the New York marriage records I found their marriage in Manhattan in March 1911. This was why their names had not appeared in the 1911 England census.

Mark's photograph of them was clearly their wedding portrait taken in New York, and on closer inspection I could see the wedding ring on Blanche's left hand. What was less obvious was that she was two months pregnant, so they must have returned to Britain for the birth of their son seven months later. Unfortunately, their baby boy died in infancy, but following the First World War – where Fred served on the Western Front – Blanche and Fred went on to have three daughters, the youngest of whom, Diane, was born in 1930 in Dorchester, where the family had a grocery shop.

Mark has always believed that his flair for retail comes from the genes of his maternal grandparents, even though he never actually met his grocer grandfather Fred, who died suddenly in 1938. If the shop was still standing in South Street, Dorchester, I'm sure Mark would have bought it by now and opened a Lush shop by way of a memorial to his maternal grandparents.

There is no doubt that Blanche was very influential in Mark's upbringing, and her house was a happy home for a growing boy. She was always there for him when he came home from school, helping him with his homework and encouraging him to join the church and school choirs and enter singing competitions. She had music qualifications herself so it must have been a great joy for her to watch her grandson singing.

Nan, as Mark called his grandmother, had Mark all to herself – and he had her all to himself – from 1954 until 1964 when Diane decided to remarry. It was not a marriage of which Blanche approved; Eric was Blanche's lodger, a committed bachelor in his late thirties, and young Mark had already been on the receiving end of his hand. The thought of Eric becoming Mark's stepfather filled both grandmother and grandson with dread – they had a strong bond and parting was going to hurt.

Today, a twelve-year-old boy would know all about his parents' divorce and would probably have a say in the matter, but in 1964 divorce was still something of a taboo. Unknown to Mark, Eric had in fact sought out John Constantine by visiting his parents in Manchester, and discovered that John was living in Gloucestershire with Prudence Marston Brogan, a young British woman whom he had 'rescued' from a bad marriage in Kenya. Her father had been the town clerk of a provincial town north of Nairobi and it appears that John had become acquainted with them while serving in the Royal Kenyan Police.

Diane needed a divorce to marry Eric, and John needed a divorce to marry Prudence, and so the deed was done, with little reference to Mark. He wasn't told where his father was living and John made no attempt to see his son, unless he did so quietly and from a distance. Somehow I doubt that because, had John Constan-

CIRCA 1950

Mark's father (right) on a fishing trip

tine seen his twelve-year-old son in 1964, he would have recognised a mirror image of himself at the same age and this whole story would surely have turned out differently.

Both couples were remarried within a few months of each other and, while Diane took the name of her new husband, Mark kept his father's surname despite having no idea of his Constantine family heritage. The only tangible reminders he had of his father were two black-and-white photographs – one of his father on a fishing trip, and the other as a newborn baby in his father's arms – two precious photographs that Mark kept safely throughout his life.

If being separated from his Nan and moving into a new home with his mother and stepfather was hard for Mark, worse was to follow. Within a few months, in October 1964, Blanche died and was cremated without fuss in Weymouth Crematorium. Mark, her only grandchild, was not taken to her funeral; nor was there any memorial for him to visit. She just disappeared from his life.

Mark was traumatised by the loss of his grandmother. When he developed chest pains some months after her death, he was diagnosed with pleurisy but was convinced he was going to die from a heart attack as his Nan had done. He desperately needed the love and structure in his life that she had always provided, and he couldn't cope with a stepfather who was short on empathy and big on discipline. As a result, there began years of teenage angst directed at his mother and stepfather, blaming them, and even himself, for breaking Nan's heart. Grief manifested as troublesome behaviour. The choirboy became a rebel and it would take a very long time for Mark to lay the ghost of his grandmother's death to rest.

# <u>03</u> Homeless

As the new decade began, Mark and I settled into a year of coming of age, both convinced that we had found the loves of our lives and equally certain that in a few short years we would leave for London and make our fortunes. With my blonde hair now down past my shoulders and a camera slung around my neck, I certainly looked like an art student but, in truth, a keen interest in the cinema was no substitute for understanding art and composition not to mention the physics of light refraction.

Because Mo lived in Dorchester and I was in Bournemouth five days a week, Mark and I often wouldn't see each other for weeks on end. It was a hell of a journey from his house to hers, a sixteen-mile round trip, which he mainly did by bike, or by bike and train when the weather was really wet.

Now that winter had set in, Mark's Man With No Name poncho had been replaced by a military greatcoat, which he certainly needed to keep warm during his travels. In fact, he had worn the greatcoat throughout his final winter at school and was often seen on the back of a motor scooter driven by his classmate, Mick Emery, coat-tails flying in the wind. Tragically, Mick had an accident, which he survived, but his pillion-passenger that day – Perry Stevens, another member of form 5X – was killed aged just seventeen. Since that day, Mark has never got behind the handlebars of a motor scooter or the wheel of a car. He cycles, catches a train, or takes a taxi, in that order.

One day in late summer he turned up at my house, looking a bit the worse for wear, only to inform me that he had left home and was now living in the woods near Mo's house. He'd had yet another blazing argument with his mother and stepfather and came home one evening to find himself locked out of his own house. Exactly which evening this happened he never said, as he had been trying to keep the whole thing a secret for some time and had been crashing with a work colleague or friends at Weymouth Drama Club – and more recently co-habiting with Brer Rabbit.

I was never a witness to the altercations that Mark had with his mother and stepfather, as I never got past the doorstep. It was not a house that you were ever invited into. Mark told me that most arguments were over money, in particular the lack of contribution from him to the family finances. As a hairdressing apprentice, he took home only £3 a week in the first year, yet his mother had been left over £1,000 in her mother's will (the equivalent of around £20,000 today) and Mark never saw a penny of that. I was on a student bursary and had some income from a part-time job, yet my parents never asked me for money while I was in further education.

In 1967, Diane and Eric had a baby daughter who they named Laura. Mark remembers changing her nappies and walking her in the pram with the girl from next door. He described her as a sunny baby full of life with whom he would dance endlessly to the tune of *Round and Round* by the Panama Jug Band.

Now, almost three years after Laura's arrival, Mark's situation had deteriorated to the point where he was living in a bivouac made out of tree branches, and he would sleep there after leaving Mo's house in the evening. Every morning Mark would cycle into Weymouth, change his clothes and clean himself up at the salon before anyone arrived, desperate that his boss should not find out that he was homeless. Nan would have turned in her grave if she hadn't been cremated.

When I told my parents of Mark's circumstances they immediately offered him the spare room in our house, now that my sister was married and had moved out. They did not hesitate, despite the fact that my father and Mark's stepfather knew each other well through church. First and foremost, my father was a Christian, a true Samaritan, and he knew that whatever problems Mark had, they weren't going to be solved by him living rough. So Mark moved in with us – Mum, Dad, me and Timmy the cat. Timmy was on his last legs, though, and tended to leave little piles or puddles behind the sofa or other discreet places around the house. Mum worked from 6pm to 10pm in a local factory and so it often fell to me to clean up after Timmy with newspaper. Often Dad would be reading his *Dorset Evening Echo* at the dining table in the kitchen, only to discover a few pages were missing; he knew what had happened and he would snarl 'Bloody cat.'

This routine was new to our eighteen-year-old lodger, and when Mark accidently knocked tea over the *Echo* one night while dunking biscuits, he screwed up the newspaper and put it in the waste bin. When Dad came home from work, he looked for his *Evening Echo* and must have eventually found it in the bin. Mark and I were in the lounge and all we could hear was 'Bloody cat!' Mark almost wet himself laughing as poor Timmy was blamed when, for once, he was entirely innocent.

Fun though it was, it was clear that Mark was too independent to lodge with us permanently. Besides, as we lived next to the post office, he was sure to bump into his mother or stepfather at some point. He was never going to return home, that was certain, but my parents' kindness bought him some time until a friend offered him a tiny holiday let for the winter once the summer season had come to an end. Even this arrangement was never going to work long term, and eventually Mo's father, who was a member of the Freemasons, used his connections to put Mark in contact with a charity called the Gordon Boys' Messenger Corps.

Gordon Boys, as the name suggests, was founded by General Gordon of Khartoum. It began as orphanages or homes for parentless boys, and they were run in a military style with the boys wearing uniforms. Similar to the Boys' Brigade, the Gordon Boys had their own national structure and marching bands, and evolved into the Gordon Boys' Messenger Corps, which provided work for the boys in delivering telegrams and postal messages. By 1970 the Gordon

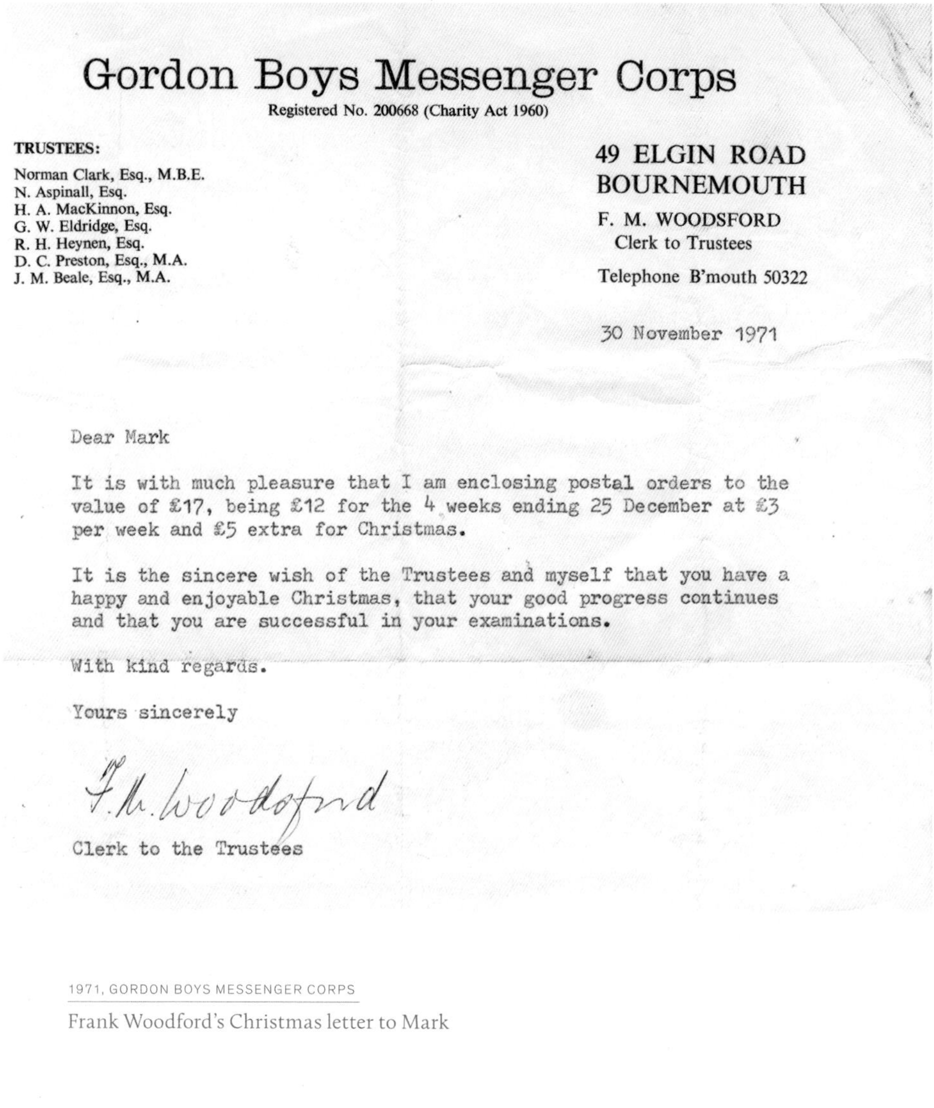

# Gordon Boys Messenger Corps
### Registered No. 200668 (Charity Act 1960)

**TRUSTEES:**
Norman Clark, Esq., M.B.E.
N. Aspinall, Esq.
H. A. MacKinnon, Esq.
G. W. Eldridge, Esq.
R. H. Heynen, Esq.
D. C. Preston, Esq., M.A.
J. M. Beale, Esq., M.A.

**49 ELGIN ROAD**
**BOURNEMOUTH**

F. M. WOODSFORD
Clerk to Trustees

Telephone B'mouth 50322

30 November 1971

Dear Mark

It is with much pleasure that I am enclosing postal orders to the value of £17, being £12 for the 4 weeks ending 25 December at £3 per week and £5 extra for Christmas.

It is the sincere wish of the Trustees and myself that you have a happy and enjoyable Christmas, that your good progress continues and that you are successful in your examinations.

With kind regards.

Yours sincerely

*F. M. Woodsford*

Clerk to the Trustees

1971, GORDON BOYS MESSENGER CORPS
Frank Woodford's Christmas letter to Mark

Boys had ceased to be a messenger service, but the charity was still helping lost and orphaned boys to stay on the straight and narrow, and it was at this point that Frank Woodsford entered Mark's life.

I never met Frank, but he was the man who introduced Mark to the true meaning of the word 'charity.' After meeting Mark and hearing of his fairly dire financial and domestic circumstances, Frank arranged for him to receive a monthly allowance from the Gordon Boys until he completed his hairdressing apprenticeship. It was £12 a month, which doesn't sound much now but back then it was enough for Mark to rent a room in Chelmsford Street in Weymouth, in a house run by a lady from the Salvation Army. It was all very strict, and the rules were even pinned to the wall: no girlfriends in the room, or even the building, and no smoking or drinking alcohol. For Mark, the financial support he received from the Gordon Boys was a lifeline, as he could not survive on his apprenticeship wages alone. Mark would have regular meetings with Frank, and at Christmas the Gordon Boys would send a little bonus – an extra couple of quid as a seasonal gesture of goodwill – which Mark found hard to believe when it first happened. I remember him telling me that he just burst into tears when he got the postal order. Many years later, Frank invited Mark to become a trustee of the Gordon Boys, and Mark was happy to repay his debt to the charity many times over.

Today Mark and his company are famous for supporting small charities, where a little money goes a long way. He has been accused of using his wealth to fund anarchists and anti-establishment groups, but these charges are just cheap headlines. He does give to small organisations that seek to protect wildlife, the environment and human rights, but only in modest amounts, where the money makes an immediate difference and avoids the overheads of large charities. It's a lesson that he learned as a beneficiary of the Gordon Boys and it's a lesson he has never forgotten.

1972, WHOLESALE BILL FORM THE NEWSAGENT

Mark's second job

Charity helped pay the bills but, apart from the Christmas bonus, there wasn't a lot left over for buying records and having fun. A second job was needed and the Osment household was the home of second and even third jobs. Ever since I can remember, my father always had extra jobs. Although he worked Monday to Friday reading meters for the Electricity Board, on Sundays he bought and sold newspapers. I think he inherited this little sideline from a workmate, but in any case it involved going to the railway station very early on a Sunday morning, buying newspapers from the agent at a trade price, and then selling them to customers at the retail price printed on the newspaper. Dad started out using a large butcher's bike with a huge front carrier, and he gradually built up a newspaper round that stretched through the vast swathes of council estates on the Westham side of Weymouth. When the enterprise became too much for a bike, he brought in a partner with a three-wheeler Reliant Regal. When I reached eleven years of age he inducted me into the business too – first with a canvas newspaper-bag, which I used to refill from the butcher's bike, and later from the Reliant, at which point I got to have the butcher's bike and my own news-paper round.

Every Sunday it took me the best part of five hours as I went house to house, picking up money from under mats and pots, and shoving the papers through letterboxes. It was hard work but it was only one morning each week, and we made good money; hence the reason why I was still doing it at eighteen years of age, although by then I wasn't overly keen on being called 'the paperboy', particularly by a couple of girls who I had known from my schooldays who would come to the door in their nighties just to tease me. Dad, though, had been doing it a lot longer than me and was ready to retire. All we needed was someone reliable who wanted to earn some extra money.

The job was tailor-made for Mark. Chelmsford Street was practically next to the railway station, and I was happy to loan him the butcher's bike so that I could move up to the Reliant Regal. I told him that he'd have to learn all the addresses and which papers they took by heart: *Pic, Pic n' People, Pic n' News* (the *Sunday Mirror* had ceased to be called the *Sunday Pictorial* for many years, but we in the trade still called it 'the *Pic*'). Surprisingly, for someone not best known for early rising in those days, Mark took to the job well and we'd meet up at my house for tea and biscuits at the end of our rounds on a Sunday and quickly empty my mother's cut-glass biscuit barrel. After my parents died in 2007 and 2008 I gave Mark the

2018, POOLE

My mother's biscuit barrel on Mark's mantlepiece

biscuit barrel, which he keeps on the mantlepiece in his kitchen. We still chew the cud over a cup of tea and biscuits from my mother's biscuit barrel whenever I drop into his house.

My time at art college was one of the happiest periods of my life and while initially I struggled with photography, I took to film-making like a duck to water. Even the great Ken Russell, who was renowned for being a hugely artistic director, wrote in his autobiography, *A British Picture*, that film production is ninety per cent organisation and ten per cent inspiration. It turned out that I was a natural at logistics and my directorial debut came quickly, in the first few weeks of my second year.

Having learned the basics of establishing shot, mid-shot and close-up, we were given a 100 feet roll of 16mm black and white film, and told to make a short silent movie about anything to do with trains. As someone who commuted to college every day, I came up with a boy-meets-girl story that appealed to my romantic side.

```
EXT: BOURNEMOUTH STATION: DAY

Boy sat on a bench waiting for a train on down platform sees
beautiful girl sitting on bench waiting for a train on the up
platform. They exchange flirtatious looks and the boy imagines
marrying the girl in a dream sequence where, in slow-motion, they
run up the steps of the iron footbridge over the old Victorian
railway station and meet in a loving embrace, before a railway
porter wearing a dog collar performs their marriage.
```

A very Ken Russell moment I thought, and maybe a bit ambitious for my first short film, but I loved pulling together all the elements – the script, the crew, the cast, the location, and best of all telling a story in pictures. Also it was quite cool to be the person that calls 'Action!'

Back in Weymouth, Mark was now quite independent, thanks to his Gordon Boys monthly postal orders and the Sunday-paper business. A year into his hairdressing apprenticeship, and always the entrepreneur, he persuaded me to take photographs of all the stylists, to put on display outside the entrance of the salon, as it was situated over a shop. No money changed hands but it introduced me to a group of mini-skirted hairdressers who were keen to get their scissors working on my long blonde hair. That was how the mullet came about and it took ages to grow out.

Mark was also a rising star in the Weymouth Drama Club, having done some voluntary work experience with their chief make-up artist, Jack Edwards, who was also the county youth employment officer. Mark had taken on a few roles following his abrupt depar-ture from the church drama

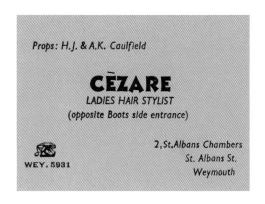

Props: H.J. & A.K. Caulfield

# CĒZARE
### LADIES HAIR STYLIST
#### (opposite Boots side entrance)

WEY. 5931

2, St.Albans Chambers
St. Albans St.
Weymouth

1970, WEYMOUTH

Mark's hairdressing salon business card

group two years earlier, and as good-looking eighteen-year-old boys didn't generally join drama societies, he was in great demand. The fact that he could also cut hair and do make-up was an added bonus for the Weymouth thespians, and for many years Mark spent a lot of time in their company.

Given the numbers of girls and women in the town who had their hair or make-up fashioned by Mark in the course of his job and hobby, it was amazing that he did not succumb to temptation

1969, WEYMOUTH PAVILION

Mark in Weymouth Drama Club production of *Not in the Book*

but remained true to his now steady girl-friend Mo, and she to him. He had plenty of offers – all the more so now that he was getting speaking and even singing parts in these local productions which played at the Pavilion theatre every May and November. *Lock Up Your Daughters* was a particularly fruity production, with Mark cast as the dashing Captain Constant. Forget internet dating; just join your local Am Dram Society if you are looking for close encounters with the opposite, or even same sex.

Mark has always had the ability to test the staying power of the people closest to him, and Mo, Geri and I would loyally watch whatever production he was starring in, until he took on a role in *The Entertainer.* John Osborne's three-act play is not one for the faint-hearted, even with Lawrence Olivier in the lead role of Archie Rice. For an amateur company it's theatrical suicide as there's not a lot of laughs – or indeed anything to get excited about unless you are a theatre connoisseur. And so it proved. On the opening night at Weymouth Pavilion there were fewer than fifty people in the audience, and after the interval there were less than ten and three of them were Mo, Geri and me. Mark had the fairly small part of Frank Rice, although it did include a singing solo, and there were long waits to endure between his appearances on stage.

**WEYMOUTH DRAMA CLUB**
presents
**'THE ENTERTAINER'**
by John Osborne
at the PAVILION THEATRE
**MAY 25th — 26th & 27th at 7.45 p.m.**

This ticket is available for any performance, but must be exchanged at the Weymouth Pavilion Box Office for a numbered Reserved Seat. Theatre Box Office opens on Saturday, 20th May.

**Telephone Bookings must be claimed before 7 p.m. on day of performance.**

**Admission 30p**

1972, WEYMOUTH PAVILION
Ticket to *The Entertainer*

It was sheer purgatory – enough to end a relationship, let alone a friendship – but somehow we all survived, and the four of us would often sit around in pubs, gradually formulating a plan for moving to London once Mark had completed his apprenticeship and I had graduated from art college. We still had over a year to go, however, learning our respective trades. Geri and I got free hair trims, Mo and Mark got free photographs, and we met regularly to play board games, particularly *Risk*, which Mark and I had started playing when he came to live with us. It would become an obsession, and lead onto bigger things, but when we were not all together, Mark and Mo spent a lot of time in the woods getting up close with nature, while Geri and I spent a lot of time in the cinema just getting up close.

We were all blissfully unaware that 250 miles away in Barton, Manchester, a sixty-five-year-old retired miner had recently passed away. His name was John Hyde Constantine, grandfather of apprentice hairdresser Mark Constantine.

# <u>04</u> Flatmates

By May 1972 much water had passed under the bridge. Mark was approaching the end of his apprenticeship in September and I was just eight weeks away from leaving Bournemouth & Poole College of Art with my Diploma in Art & Design (Film). We had all discussed the 'leaving Weymouth' plan many times, and decided I would have to be in the vanguard as I needed to find a job in the film industry in London. Mark had now made up his mind that he wouldn't be pursuing a career as a make-up artist at the BBC; instead he wanted to become a top London stylist and was applying to the best salons in the West End.

However, finding any job in the British TV or film industry proved much harder than I had envisaged, as a powerful trade union, the ACTT (Associated Cinematograph and Television Technicians), ran a closed shop and obtaining union membership was very restricted. Things became more urgent when Mark had an interview with the Elizabeth Arden salon in Bond Street and got offered a job as a first-year stylist, called an 'improver' in the trade. Elizabeth Arden was a Canadian businesswoman who died in 1966 but had made her fortune in the American cosmetics industry. Her unique selling point was teaching women how to apply make-up, and she pioneered such concepts as the scientific formulation of cosmetics, beauty makeovers, and coordinating colours of eye, lip and facial make-up. It was a job made in heaven for Mark – a company that offered mainly rich, middle-aged women the complete hair and beauty experience. Who better to make these wealthy London socialites feel younger and more beautiful than a handsome young man who would happily flirt with them, and maybe earn a tip for himself in the process? But it meant that now there was a deadline of mid-September for me to find a job.

It was my sister who eventually came to my rescue. Her next-door neighbour's mother, known as Mrs C due to her unpronounceable Polish surname, managed the restaurant in the Science Museum in London. She was happy to give me part-time work while I continued my job search in the capital. It didn't pay me enough to get a flat, but I had about four weeks' start on Mark's arrival.

When you've studied photography and film for three years it's quite dispiriting to be shown how to spread butter onto bread and scrape it off again by a barely sober Irishman. I didn't really know what a casual worker was, but I soon found out, as Michael regaled me with the story of his life on the mean streets of London. Sometimes he would disappear for days on end and then turn up looking like he had been kicked down the Seven Sisters Road by a bunch of football hooligans.

By the August bank holiday weekend I still hadn't found a job in the film industry and was living in digs in Palmers Green. After much soul-searching, Geri and I decided to tell Mark and Mo that we couldn't go through with the plan to get a flat together in London while I didn't have a regular job that paid sufficient money. This news didn't go down well, but after much discussion we agreed that the master plan would have to be achieved in stages. A couple of weeks later, Mark and Mo arrived in London. Mo had found a job with a legal firm in the City, and with it a flatshare with two other girls in Earls Court, but Mark was still looking. He booked himself into a seedy hostel near Kings Cross Station and experienced the worst night's sleep of his life.

Mark very quickly found a two-person bedsit in Kensington and asked me to move in with him. We met in a gay pub in Earls Court, not deliberately, but we were new to London. Quite how we ended up there, I'm not sure – maybe one of Mark's new gay colleagues at the salon had set him up. It turned out that the real reason Mark had got the job at Elizabeth Arden was because the manager and several of the male stylists fancied him. They came onto him from day one, goosing him on the stairs and pursuing him around the salon. In Weymouth the stylists were predominantly women; in the West End many of the top stylists were gay men. Indeed, homosexuality in England and Wales had only been decriminalised in 1967, and then only between consenting adults over the age of twenty-one.

Mark informed me that he had already agreed to the rent of £15.50 per week, plus halves on electricity and food, so about £10 each. I was earning only £12 a week at the Science Museum and it cost £5.50 to go home to see my girlfriend. Once again, I had to disappoint him. This time Mark got angry, and when Mark gets angry the impetuous side of his nature overrides the empathy that he normally has in abundance. If I didn't want 'in', he said, he would have to find a new flatmate, and that's exactly what he decided to do. Or at least he tried to, but he really had taken on a pricey pad. The big plan had now fallen apart completely. Mark was in Kensington, Mo was in Earl's Court, I was in Palmers Green, and Geri was still in Weymouth – all, it seemed, because I couldn't find a proper job.

Finally, I got a break. Mrs. C, bless her, told me that she knew a TV producer at the Young & Rubicam Advertising Agency from her days as manager of the staff canteen there, and she kindly offered to ring him for me. As luck would have it, they had an opening for a junior projectionist in their TV commercials department, starting immediately. As the second-largest advertising agency in the world, Y&R was a very cool place to work – and at £16 a week plus luncheon vouchers, it was a big improvement on the Science Museum restaurant. Even Mark was happy because he hadn't managed to find a flatmate and I could now move in with him, although without our girlfriends. The finances still didn't quite add up, but Mrs C said that she could always find part-time work for me at weekends, and from the bedsit in Kensington it was literally five minutes' walk to the back door of the Museum.

So far, so good, except that I only got to go home and see my soon-to-be fiancée every second weekend, while Mark and Mo – who had become engaged the previous year and even had an official photograph taken for the local newspaper – got to play husband and wife in my absence. Looking back, I think that the prospect of sharing a flat with our girlfriends was as much a motivating factor in our move to London as finding a job in our chosen careers.

1971, DORCHESTER

Mr. and Mrs. Kenyon proudly announce the engagement of their daughter Margaret Joan to Mr. Mark Constantine.

Our bedsit was in a terrace off Kensington Road, opposite Kensington Gardens; only Mark could have chosen one of the most expensive boroughs of London to live in. The Royal Albert Hall was literally on our doorstep, although we wouldn't be buying tickets for shows there any time soon. We had one large bed–sitting room on the third floor, with a small kitchenette off one end, and a little hallway leading to a decent-sized bathroom, although you had to remember to take your door key with you or leave it on the latch. The electricity was a pay-as-you-go shilling (5p) in the meter arrangement, just like home, and we had a one-bar electric fire, which we put on only when it got really cold. Our entertainment in the evening was the radio, a record player and endless games of *Risk*. There were two single beds, on opposite sides of the room, a rocking chair and two wingback armchairs that we would shove together to make a bed for Mo when she stayed over some nights.

2018, LONDON

The top floor bedsit that Mark and I shared in Kensington in 1972

I was very homesick for Geri but at least Mark and Mo didn't make things worse by cuddling up together while I was sleeping in the same room.

Our staple diet was porridge, fish fingers and whatever came out of a can, except for every second Sunday evening, when Mrs C would let me take home all the leftover food at the Science Museum restaurant so it was ready for restocking on Monday. Like two hungry lion cubs, Mark and Mo would be waiting for Sunday tea, which generally consisted of an assortment of sandwiches and large if slightly soggy slices of Black Forest gateau or strawberry cheesecake, these being the most expensive items on the Museum restaurant menu. This fortnightly feast also signalled that I had to wait only another five days to see my sweetheart in Weymouth.

Shortly after moving in with Mark, he nearly set fire to the flat. Just as when he was in Scouts, Mark did not do domestic chores. Mo and I would take the washing to the launderette each week and watch it go round for an hour. I did most of the cleaning and the cooking if Mo wasn't around, although there was a limit to what could be made on a two-ring Belling electric stove. Breakfast was porridge, which was always made by me, and as my commute to work in Camden Town was longer than Mark's, I often left him lying in bed, with his porridge on low heat. One evening I came home, opened the flat door and smelled burning. In the kitchenette I found the porridge saucepan with a hole burned through it and the wallpaper above the cooker black and smouldering. I don't know how the electricity hadn't run out, maybe we had overpaid, but the paper was only minutes from igniting.

We survived that, only for one of the flats opposite to catch fire one evening, and we had a ringside view of the fire brigade arriving to put it out. Mo found it all quite frightening, and Mark's plan to tie sheets together if it ever happened to us wasn't very reassuring. Firstly, because his knot-tying skills in Scouts had never been great, and secondly because three floors below us was a typical London iron-railing fence with spikes on the top. A fate worse than death, we all agreed.

1972, LONDON
Me at Trafalgar Square

In the Bond Street salon Mark was getting into his stride and mixing with the rich and famous. Among the salon's clients were Jackie Onassis (whose hair he washed once, I think), several leading West End actresses, members of the royal family and a socialite famous for her alleged affairs. These powerful women made a big impression on Mark and one regularly gave him free tickets to the Royal Court Theatre in Sloane Square, which was right up his street. When Mark launched his first perfume collection, in 2010 under the brand name Gorilla Perfumes, he created three limited-edition fragrances named the Heiress, the Actress, and the Duchess, all based on the smells these women evoked when he was a twenty-year-old hairdresser. I say hairdresser, but most of the time Mark was washing hair. His job hadn't progressed much from his apprenticeship days, except that the standards in London were much higher than in Weymouth. He was still privy to the kind of gossip that circulates only between clients and their hairdresser, and he probably earned more in tips than I did working all weekend at the restaurant.

I don't think Mark and Mo were overly sympathetic to my predicament. Working twelve days a fortnight to spend a weekend with my fiancée – and eight hours of that travelling – was emotionally draining. Also, I wasn't really in my ideal job. I had quickly learned to lace a Carbon Arc film projector in less than twenty seconds, and project 35mm TV commercials all day. It was fun at first, but I soon realised that being a junior projectionist would be a very slow career route. I started looking for other jobs that I could do within the agency, and volunteered to work late when the market-research people did blind tastings with members of the public – not a bad job when two of our brands were Cadbury's chocolate and Double Diamond beer.

Back at the bedsit, life continued to revolve around listening to music and playing board games in the evenings, occasionally punctuated by a free box of chocolates. We were living in swinging London, yet we hardly ever went out. I pleaded poverty and if I wasn't working every other Saturday and Sunday I was either on my way to or from Weymouth. I'm not sure what Mark and Mo got up to, but it never resulted in better meals or in me getting free tickets to go anywhere. I did watch the odd movie in Leicester Square, like Stanley Kubrick's *A Clockwork Orange*, but even these indulgences cost a small fortune – £16 doesn't go far when £12 goes on rent, living expenses and Tube fares.

One morning in December, I received a letter from my college tutor informing me that an engineering company in Bournemouth was looking to employ an in-house filmmaker. Was I interested in applying? Effectively I would be a one-man film unit, writing the scripts, and shooting and editing the films. When could I start? Monday 15th January 1973. After a tough six months in London, Christmas 1972 was going to be a very happy one. I was coming home in order to start my career again, no more seeing my fiancée every other weekend, no more porridge and fish fingers, and no more watching all my wages walk out of the door. Mark and Mo seemed quite happy too. Mo was getting fed up with her rowdy flatmates and couldn't wait to move into the bedsit with Mark.

Two weeks later, Mark and Mo came to see me off and said a teary goodbye at Waterloo station. The big plan was over – the four of us would never share a flat together in London, and before the New Year was out Mark and Mo would also leave the capital. In the meantime there were a couple of weddings and honeymoons to fit in, and Mark would make a change of direction in his career, laying the foundations for his future business. I think he knew he was not cut out to be a stylist, and he joined the Ginger Group in Knightsbridge as a trainee trichologist. We used to joke that he was a 'trick cyclist' but, whatever it was, it involved examining a client's hair and scalp condition and recommending a course of treatment, as well as attending night school and taking more exams. Among his clients was a young Anna Wintour of *Harpers & Queen* magazine, who would one day become one of the most powerful figures in the world of fashion as editor-in-chief of American *Vogue*.

The job became more difficult for Mark when the salon sacked his manager for attempting to set up a breakaway company and Mark became the resident trichologist at the age of twenty. He was on a steep learning curve, working all day and studying organic chemistry in the evenings in order to be able to formulate the in-house products that the stylists would recommend to their clients. Now it was Mark's turn to become stressed with the whole London work–life balance.

Mark and Mo's way of relaxing was youth-hostelling. I think they initially thought that cycling into the countryside and staying in youth hostels would be a way of getting quality 'alone time' together, but in those days youth hostels had separate dormitories for boys and girls. Some wardens were less strict than others, and when Mark and Mo met up with John Leadwood, the hippie warden of a hostel in the New Forest, they found a bolthole where free love and nature watching came at a very cheap price. Moreover, they found an environmental mentor who took their growing interest in flora and fauna and turned it into a lifelong passion. However, spring had not yet sprung in 1973, so it was cold winter nights in London for Mark and Mo, while I was back at home almost as if I had never left.

Soon the Easter weekend beckoned and we had arranged to spend the four-day holiday in London with Mark and Mo. On the Thursday evening we drove up in my Mini to my old bedsit in Kensington, where Mark and Mo had put up a divider screen between the two sides of the room: theirs and ours. They had also planned a weekend of arts and culture the sort of thing we should have been doing regularly had we all gone to London together eight months earlier.

First up was a new play called *Savages*, by Christopher Hampton, at the Royal Court Theatre. Next, a film I had been banging on about since art college, Alain Resnais' *Last Year at Marienabad* that was showing at the National Film Theatre on the Southbank. It's either a masterpiece or totally incomprehensible, depending on your point of view; Geri and Mo slept through most of it to the point of snoring. We also fitted in Luis Buñuel's *The Discreet Charm of the Bourgeoisie*, which was slightly easier to follow. One evening we ended up at a dilapidated if not actually derelict East End theatre to watch a Renaissance comedy 'in the round' entitled *A Chaste Maid in Cheapside* where we were seated so close to the actors that the sword-fights had an added frisson of reality. And to round off the weekend, a trip to the Dominion Cinema on Tottenham Court Road to see the film of the hit musical *Cabaret*, starring Liza Minnelli.

Mark and Mo had stocked the flat with food, wine and nibbles too. It was all such a contrast to the austerity we had endured through the winter of 1972. Late one night, after having consumed a bit too much red wine and peanuts we fell into our single bed. Geri suddenly needed the bathroom, which was through the locked front door and across the lobby. Unfortunately, she didn't make it that far, as she tripped over the coffee table, crashed through the dividing screen and promptly threw-up all over the room. It was the first time my now eighteen-year-old fiancée had ever got properly drunk . . . and the last. The embarrassment of wrecking Mark and Mo's flat has stayed with her to this day.

A couple of months after the Easter weekend Mark and Mo got married, on 2nd June 1973. Mo's parents had a large house in Dorchester, so the wedding at the village church in West Stafford was followed by a garden party at the house. Amazingly, Mark invited his mother, stepfather and seven-year-old half-sister Laura, although the family was not reconciled by any means. It was just a polite gesture, and I suspect it was actually Mark's mother-in-law,

Margery, who instigated it. Mo's parents were the epitome of British middle-class respectability, but without any affected airs and graces. Both were educated northerners; Margery was a science graduate, teacher and church organist, and Alan a civil servant and freemason. At any rate, they certainly knew how to put on a first-class wedding.

Mark insisted that I took photographs – not the formal ones but the informal ones that are so popular today: the bride getting ready and the unguarded moments. Mark's best man was Pete, his childhood friend who had lived just around the corner from him. A man of few words, Pete hadn't realised that he would have to make a speech, which left us with the best part of a twenty-minute taxi journey to the wedding to write one for him. A veteran of many family weddings, and now an up-and-coming scriptwriter, I scribbled down a basic best man's speech – who to thank and so on – then advised him that Mark would probably say how lovely the bridesmaids looked, while Pete should begin by thanking Mark on their behalf.

1973, WEST STAFFORD, DORSET

Mark and Mo's official wedding photograph

He read it verbatim, without a pause, delivering what must have been one of the shortest best man's speeches ever. There wasn't a single joke or any of the usual embarrassing anecdotes of the bridegroom's bachelorhood. Maybe that's why Mark chose him, because there was plenty of ammunition for a more eloquent best man!

Mark and Mo's wedding was a very elegant affair; a pretty village church followed by a very English garden party with tea and cakes and cucumber sandwiches. There might have been a pianist in the marquee, but there certainly wasn't a disco to

disturb the residents of leafy Dorchester. As Mark and Mo's big day drew to a close, we all gathered at Dorchester South station to wave the bride and groom off on their honeymoon, Mark clutching an unopened set of sheets and pillowcases they intended to take with them to their honeymoon cottage in Ireland the next day.

By June 1973 London was becoming the target of an IRA bombing campaign, and the windows of Mo's legal firm in the City had already been blown out by the Old Bailey bomb in March of that year. In order to get well away from an increasingly stressful lifestyle in London, the happy couple set off for County Kerry, for their romantic honeymoon in a quiet cottage where their days could be filled with cycling and nature watching.

The picturesque village of Ventry, on the Dingle Peninsula, boasted stunning scenery and seabirds galore, not to mention a quiet village pub where a young London trichologist, never shy to express an opinion, could mix with the locals and discuss the 'Troubles' over a pint of Guinness. Little did Mark realise that a pub in the heart of Republican country is not the place to talk down the IRA. At best, you'll get a quiet word in your ear; at worst a couple of locals will be waiting for you on the way home. Mark was lucky, the landlord did have a quiet word in his ear, and mentioned that the man staying with his family in the holiday cottage next door to Mark and Mo was a high-ranking member of the Provisional IRA's army council. I think

1973, DORCHESTER SOUTH STATION
Mark and Mo leaving for their honeymoon

My photographs of Mark and Mo's special day

the landlord just told Mark the man's name, and that he had only recently been released from prison. It had the desired effect. Mark and Mo spent the night at their honeymoon cottage fully dressed, wide awake and ready to leave at first light. Unfortunately the bus only ran twice a week, and they had no money to change their travel itinerary. So having put the fear of God into them, the villagers and their infamous neighbour now tried to reassure the nervous newly-weds. But even when Mark and Mo caught the train back to Cork at the end of the week, they discovered the former IRA chief and his family were making the same railway journey. The honeymoon was anything but stress free, and on their return to London Mark and Mo pondered their future, as the IRA stepped up its bombing campaign in the capital.

Back in Bournemouth I was slowly getting to grips with industrial filmmaking, using the Kodak Super 8mm format. In six months I had made one complete marketing film, and started several project case-histories, including regular visits to the Reliant factory in Tamworth. This was not to film the Reliant Regal, the car that I had driven around in to deliver Sunday newspapers, but an all new, sleeker fibreglass version, the Reliant Robin, the most popular fibreglass car ever built. I was also being introduced to the world of trade unionism and learnt some hard lessons while visiting engineering factories up and down the UK. In one factory, the production line downed tools and walked out just as I started filming, because I hadn't informed the shop steward in advance. I soon learned that the two most important people to befriend

1973, BOURNEMOUTH

The Kodak Super 8mm film format 18 frames per second

NOTICE TO STAFF

## BOMBS

Just in case - the following advice given by the Metropolitan Police and the London Fire Brigade is worth noting:

"1.  Report suspicious vehicles and objects.

2.  Find out where the suspect bomb is supposed to be.  Do not use lifts.

3.  Leave the building as safely and as quickly as possible and by the entrance farthest from where an outside bomb is reported to be.

4.  Put as many walls as possible between you and the bomb.

5.  Do not shelter near plate-glass windows.

6.  If a bomb is suspected between a quarter and half a mile away, pull down all curtains and blinds in the room.  Even net curtains can prevent flying glass from entering the room."

In the event of a bomb alarm attention should be paid to any direction to leave by the Newgate Street staircase and exit or by the Cathedral staircase and exit.

Fire Marshals for each floor should supervise the evacuation of the building.

Fs.

1973, LONDON

Mo's letter following the bombing of the Old Bailey
by the IRA

at a factory or industrial plant were the head of security and the union leader; one let you in and the other let you work. A lesson that paid dividends in years to come.

Unknown to Geri and me, Mark and Mo had reached a decision to get out of London. They had had enough of living in a bedsit, working by day, studying by night, and worrying about when and where the next bomb might go off. Geri and I found out in a strange way though. We were looking for a flat in Bournemouth to move into after our wedding in September, when we came across an advertisement in the local *Evening Echo* placed by a couple in London who were also seeking a flat in Bournemouth. The return address was familiar – it was our old bedsit in Kensington. Mischievously, Geri and I responded to the advertisement, pretending to be a wealthy old lady who lived in a large Bournemouth mansion that was far too big for her. So big that she was prepared the rent out the entire east wing. She also kept a large collection of exotic birds and needed help with them. The letter ran to a couple of pages so that Mark and Mo wouldn't get the joke until they reached the very end.

One thing Mark and I have always been good at down the years is winding each other up, but Mark will always come back with a bigger wind-up if he can. Therefore, when he told us that he had found two spanking-new flats on the same floor in Bournemouth for £22 per week, we assumed that he was having us on. Yet this time, he wasn't. Typical of Mark and Mo, they had got the train to Bournemouth one weekend without telling us, and had taken out a rental agreement on a brand-new flat on the third floor of a large Edwardian house near the railway station. We also discovered that he had got a freelance job as the resident trichologist at what was then the largest hairdressing business on the south coast, Marc Young Hairdressers, based in Poole. Mo had also found a job as secretary to the Clerk of Courts in Poole. The new flat offered storage for their bikes and tandem, and easy access to Poole or the

New Forest by train, and if we got in quick we could be their next-door neighbours. Delighted as we were to discover that Mark and Mo would be moving to Bournemouth, £22 per week seemed a bit pricey, so we continued our search for something more affordable and eventually rented the upstairs of a house in Tuckton, close to the beach at Hengistbury Head.

Before taking up residence though, we needed to get married, which we did at my parish church of St Edmunds, Weymouth. Naturally, Mark was my best man – who else would be able to embarrass me as much as possible? – with a speech that he had tastefully written on a toilet roll!

When we returned from our honeymoon in Paris, we discovered that Mark had changed his name. To avoid confusion with his boss, who also had the name Marc, Mark was required to adopt the name Matthew which, if you said it often enough and in the right voice, drove him mad. On the other hand, he and Mo have never had any qualms about constantly calling me 'Jeffrey', like I'm a naughty little boy. Far from being Mark Constantine, London stylist – or Mark Constantine, make-up artist to the stars – he was now plain 'Matthew' the salon trichologist.

Shortly after Christmas, Geri and I came home one evening to find our shared house overrun with teenagers having a party, throwing up in our bathroom and trying to gain access to our bedroom. The next day, we handed the landlady our keys and moved into a furnished ground-floor flat in Bournemouth, two floors below Mr and Mrs Constantine. It had taken nearly eighteen months, but finally we all ended up living together in the same building. Having turned down the opportunity of moving into a bright new top-floor flat on the landing opposite Mark and Mo five months earlier, we now had to settle for the older, darker and damper flat on the ground floor. Our kitchen wastes were connected by a shared plumbing system so that when Mo sang at her sink, we could hear her voice reverberating from our kitchen sink plughole. We were paying only £18 per week, which reflected the older nature of our accommodation, and explained why we spent more time in their flat than they did in ours.

And then the lights went out. On 31st December 1973 Britain began the three-day week. Rising inflation and a cap on public-sector pay precipitated industrial action by the National Union of Miners. To conserve coal stocks and maintain essential electricity supply, Prime Minister Edward Heath brought in measures restricting commercial business to three consecutive days of power per week. Television stopped broadcasting at 10.30pm, pubs shut early, and street lights were turned off.

Ahead of us lay three months of darkness, short working hours, low wages and endless board games. We did have a TV in our flat but Mark and Mo were now beginning to settle into their alternative lifestyle, one that did not require cars or televisions, just a bike and a knowledge of mushrooms and other edible wild plants.

It was the beginning of 1974 and Mark and I were both twenty-one, both married to our long-time girlfriends, and both trying to make our career choices bear fruit – in Mark's case quite literally, although he was still a little way off boiling elderflowers in a saucepan.

1973, WEYMOUTH

Mark giving the Best Man's speech at our wedding

# <u>05</u> John Hyde Constantine

To pick up the trail of Mark's father, I had to travel back in time to discover where he came from and whether he still had any living relatives who could shed some light on this elusive man. In October 2011, I only had two pieces of information that I knew to be correct: Mark's anecdotal story of his father joining the Royal Kenyan Police in 1954, and the unequivocal fact that he married Diane Gardner in Weymouth in 1950.

I typed this information into the search engine of the ancestry website and instantly found the public record of their marriage. You can't read these documents online but you can order a copy from the Public Record Office for £10.

Four days later a copy of John and Diane Constantine's marriage certificate arrived in the post, confirming their marriage details and also providing me with the names of their respective fathers, and their occupations. I already knew that Mark's maternal grandfather, Fred Gardner, a grocer, had died in 1938, but now I knew that Mark's paternal grandfather was a stoker called John Hyde Constantine, something that Mark did not know. For the next nine months, unknown to Mark or anyone else except my wife, I lived a nightly vicarious existence as I gradually unraveled the Constantine family history.

When Mark was locked out of his home at the age of 17, he never went back, despite his mother, stepfather and half-sister Laura being invited to his wedding in 1973. It was a sixteen-year-old Laura who started the long process of reconciliation between Mark and his mother, which took many years. Through Laura, I could have approached Mark's eighty-two-year-old mother Diane and asked her to cooperate in tracing Mark's family history but I wasn't sure how she would react to me digging up the past. If she hadn't told her own son, why would she tell me? After some consideration, I decided I would not risk telling anyone anything until I was sure it was the right thing to do or I had reached a complete dead end.

Using the 1911 census return, I was able to establish that Mark's grandfather John Hyde Constantine came from a mining area called Tyldesley on the outskirts of Manchester, now part of

CERTIFIED COPY OF AN ENTRY OF MARRIAGE          GIVEN AT THE GENERAL REGISTER OFFICE

Application Number  3864209/1

| No. | When Married | Name and Surname | Age | Condition | Rank or Profession | Residence at the time of Marriage | Father's Name and Surname | Rank or Profession of Father |
|---|---|---|---|---|---|---|---|---|
| 8 | November 11th 19 50 | John Constantine | 21 | Bachelor | Police Constable | 1 Ramsgate Street Dalston E 8 | John Hyde Constantine | Stoker |
| | | Diane Merrill Gardner | 20 | Spinster | Shorthand Typist | 21 Broughton Crescent Wyke Regis | Frederick Gardner (Deceased) | |

1950. Marriage solemnized at the Parish Church in the Parish of Wyke Regis in the County of Dorset

Married in the said Church according to the Rites and Ceremonies of the Church of England by or after Banns by me,

This Marriage was solemnized between us: John Constantine / Diane Merrill Gardner in the Presence of us: E. L. Bartlett / B. Gardner          F. E. Pratt (Rector)

CERTIFIED to be a true copy of an entry in the certified copy of a register of Marriages in the Registration District of **Weymouth**
Given at the GENERAL REGISTER OFFICE, under the Seal of the said Office, the  **23rd**  day of  **February**  **2012**

1950, ALL SAINTS, WYKE REGIS, WEYMOUTH
Marriage certificate of John Constantine and Diane Gardner

Greater Manchester. He was six years old in 1911 and lived with his father, Thomas Henry Constantine, and four older siblings, Ernest, Harry, Elsie and May. No mother was named, but they did have a housekeeper. I checked the 1901 census and this time found Mark's great-grandmother, Mary, together with her husband, Thomas, and her two eldest children living at the same address. I later discovered she had died in 1908, shortly after the birth of a sixth child, hence the need for Thomas to hire a housekeeper.

Mark's great-grandfather, Thomas Henry – sometimes referred to as Thomas Hyde – was a cabinetmaker and had four brothers and one sister; all were the children of Robert Constantine, who was a French-polisher. Mark has a keen eye for individual pieces

CENSUS OF ENGLAND AND WALES, 1911.

| NAME AND SURNAME | RELATIONSHIP to Head of Family | Age of Males | Age of Females | PARTICULARS as to MARRIAGE | | | PROFESSION or OCCUPATION | | | | BIRTHPLACE of every person | | NATIONALITY | INFIRMITY |
|---|---|---|---|---|---|---|---|---|---|---|---|---|---|---|
| Thos H. Constantine | Head | 40 | | Widower | 6 | 6 | Carpenter | 210 | L. & N. W. Ry Co | Worker | Cheshire Stockport | 127 | | L. & N. W. Ry |
| Mary Toney | Housekeeper | | 60 | Widow | | | | 010 | | | Lancashire [illegible] | 059 | | |
| Ernest Constantine | Son | 17 | | Single | | | Coal Mine Hewer | 150 | | Worker | Cheshire Stockport | 123 | | |
| Elsie Constantine | Daughter | | 11 | | | | School | 390 | | | Cheshire Stockport | | | |
| Harry Constantine | Son | 9 | | | | | School | | | | Cheshire Stockport | | | |
| May Constantine | Daughter | | 8 | | | | School | | | | Cheshire Stockport | | | |
| John Hyde Constantine | Son | 6 | | | | | School | | | | Lancashire Tyldesley | | | |

Signature Thomas Henry Constantine

Postal Address 11 Ashwell St. Tyldesley. Lancs.

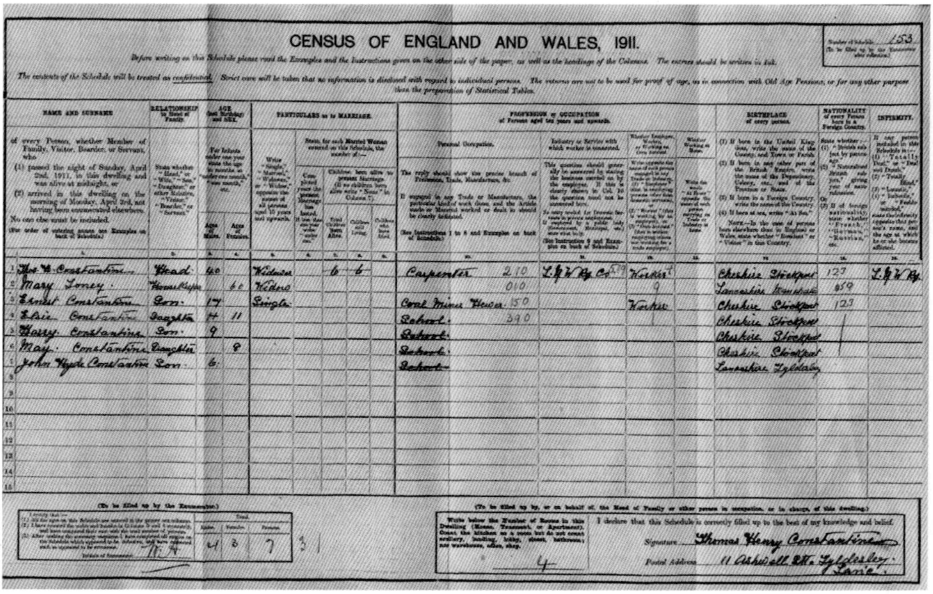

1911, TYLDESLEY, MANCHESTER

Census of England and Wales

of furniture, which would surely have pleased his first and second great-grandfathers.

Through the census returns and parish records, I was able to trace the Constantine family tree back to around 1797, beyond which things started to get a bit complicated. One thing for sure was that the Tyldesley area of Manchester was positively teeming with Constantines and Hyde Constantines in the nineteenth and early-twentieth centuries. However, I was looking for living relatives, a cousin or someone who knew John Constantine.

All of the children of Ernest, Harry, Elsie and May would be cousins of Mark's father but I was only able to trace Ernest's family line through the Hyde Constantine connection to three sisters living in Australia. Like Mark, they were all great-grandchildren of Thomas Henry Constantine, but they had no knowledge of the family history as their father, Douglas Hyde Constantine, had emigrated to Australia shortly after the Second World War.

I looked in vain for Mark's great-uncle Harry, but he had been christened Henry Bailey Constantine, an odd deviation from Hyde Constantine that had resulted from a paternal grandmother keeping

1940, EAST LANCASHIRE REGIMENT

John Hyde Constantine,
Mark's paternal grandfather

her maiden name. A long search for the marriages of great-aunts Elsie and May Constantine also yielded no results.

Mark's grandfather John Hyde Constantine was still my only lead, so I looked for and found his marriage to Matilda Bridge on Christmas Eve 1927. Mark's father, John Constantine, was born a year later, in December 1928. Mark had always told me that his father was an only child, but still I checked to see if I could find any brothers or sisters. No brothers came to light but I found two women born in the 1930s, Brenda and Margaret Constantine, whose mother's maiden name was Bridge. This was a very exciting discovery – two potential aunts – so I sent for their birth certificates.

Genealogy is all about checking the facts, and the details on Brenda and Margaret's birth certificates were unexpected. Their father was a George Constantine, a cousin of Mark's grandfather; their mother, Doris Bridge, was the sister of Mark's paternal grandmother, Matilda. To make things more confusing, Matilda and Doris lived next door to each other. Nevertheless, it seemed likely that these two close cousins of Mark's father, living in the same semi-detached house, would have been like sisters to him and they would surely know the family history. I traced their marriages but discovered, sadly, that they had both died in the last ten years. Although I could try to track down their husbands and children, it would be a long shot at best. It was a disappointing end to my search.

Wherever I looked, I found either dead ancestors or living ones so far removed that they knew nothing about the family of John Constantine. By May 2012 – after seven months of searching, and with 21st July and Mark's sixtieth birthday approaching – it was time to get all the important family records together and assemble them in a binder. I had all of the birth and marriage certificates but I had not bothered with death certificates, until now.

Initially, I requested only the death certificates of Mark's maternal grandparents. Mark has a bit of a phobia about hospitals, illness and drugs, and has used homeopathic medicines and remedies most of his life. I knew that Mark was interested in finding out if his maternal grandfather, Fred Gardner, had died of a heart condition, but the death certificate had the cause of death as a pulmonary embolism. What interested me more was the fact that his death in 1938 had not been registered by his wife but by one of his daughters. A little light flicked on in my brain: if John Constantine had never come back from Africa, and he was an only son, who had

registered the deaths of his father and his mother? I forked out
another twenty quid and sent for the death certificates of Mark's
paternal grandparents.

The deaths of Mark's grandparents tell a sad story. John Hyde
Constantine died in 1970, when Mark was eighteen, having never
met his grandson other than as a baby. Mark's grandmother Matilda
lived until 1988 and yet she also never saw him beyond his second
birthday, and so had not been present at his wedding in 1973 or
known of the birth of her great-grandsons, Simon and Jack. This was
a lady who also never saw her only son again after he left England
in 1969. Eighteen years without physical contact with her family
must have been heartbreaking and I was keen to know who had
registered her death and made the arrangements for her funeral.

It was no great surprise to discover that Mark's grandfather had
died of a long-term mining-related illness and that his death in 1970
had been registered by his wife. But when I read Matilda's death certificate, the hairs on the back of my neck literally stood up. A lady called
June Howarth had registered the death in 1988, and the relationship
to the deceased written on the death certificate read 'Daughter.'

How could I have missed this? I checked and rechecked the birth
records for every year that Matilda could possibly have conceived
a child, and found no record for the birth of a June Constantine. I
came to the conclusion that she must have been adopted – perhaps
an orphaned war baby. I looked for her marriage certificate and
quickly found the wedding record of June Constantine and Richard
Howarth, in 1963. This had to be her, but I needed to be sure. Once
again I paid my £10 and waited for the marriage certificate to arrive.
Four days later I was positively shaking when I read the details of her
marriage. Her father was named as John Hyde Constantine, retired
miner, and June had been born in 1945. Mark's long-lost Aunty June,
his father's sister, was only sixty-seven – and this time I was certain
she was very much alive.

QBDY 790882

*Application Number* 4039223/2

## CERTIFIED COPY OF AN ENTRY

| DEATH | Entry No. **235** |
|---|---|

Registration district Salford.

Sub-district Salford. Metropolitan District of Salford.

1. Date and place of death Sixteenth January 1988
Salford Royal Hospital Salford

2. Name and surname Matilda CONSTANTINE

3. Sex Female

4. Maiden surname of woman who has married BRIDGE

5. Date and place of birth 23rd October 1905. Farnworth, Bolton.

6. Occupation and usual address Widow of John Hyde CONSTANTINE Coal Miner (retired) 3 Pennington Close, Little Hulton.

7.(a) Name and surname of informant June HOWARTH

(b) Qualification Daughter.

(c) Usual address 105 Manchester Road West, Little Hulton. Manchester

8. Cause of death
1a Left lower lobe Pneumonia.
b Immobility
II Left Ventricular failure and Chronic Anaemia. (17)

Certified by M J Garton MB BS

9. I certify that the particulars given by me above are true to the best of my knowledge and belief...... J. Howarth...... Signature of informant

10. Date of registration Nineteenth January 1988

11. Signature of registrar M Paton Deputy Registrar

SEVENTEEN MR

Death certificate of Mark's grandmother Matilda Constantine

# <u>06</u> Waterloo

The three-day week ensured that 1974 got off to a very gloomy start. Filmmaking at my engineering firm had all but stopped, and with the departure of the assistant to the advertising manager I was given some of his jobs, like proofreading and print-progressing.

Mark didn't have it much better. While the salon in Poole's Arndale Centre was swanky enough for 'Matthew' the new trichologist to ply his trade, his workroom – the place where he cooked up the shampoos, conditioners and treatments sold by the salon – was located somewhere in the depths of the building, between the air-conditioning ducts and the wiring, where daylight never penetrated. It was the sort of place where the heroes of thriller films get chased by terminators. Indeed Mark almost terminated himself one day when he spilt a bottle of formaldehyde in his airless laboratory and had to quickly escape the killer gas.

Neither of our workplace scenarios had been envisaged eighteen months earlier when we had set out for London to seek fame and fortune in our chosen careers. It was clear now that, whatever the future held for us, it was going to be a slog, but we could at least console ourselves with the knowledge that every day we could go home to our comfortable furnished flats in leafy Bournemouth and spend as much 'alone time' as we could ever want with our lovely young wives.

As usual, Mark took the lead in finding whatever the town had to offer two newly married couples, and he headed straight for what he knew best: amateur dramatics. He had found an advert for the Bournemouth Little Theatre Club, which was starting a drama workshop for young actors.

The BLTC, as it was known, had been founded in 1919, and by 1931 the club had built the 450-seat Palace Court Theatre in Hinton Road with funds from shareholding members. In its heyday the BLTC had 1,500 members and hosted nine plays a year as well as touring professional repertory companies. However, by 1969, declining audiences meant the upkeep of the theatre had proved too much, and in 1971 the shareholders sold the theatre and moved into temporary rented space above a car showroom. Clearly, someone had decided an injection of young blood was required to lift the spirits of the elders who had lost their cherished theatre, although they still held on to a few of their traditions.

On a dark winter's night, we marched into the BLTC green room in jeans and sweaters to discover a fully licensed bar and a barmaid who, judging by her vintage, might well have been running the Palace Court green room since 1931. There were rules in the green room about dress code, loud talking and not mentioning the Scottish play, all of which were lost on us. Mo and Geri were not overly keen on getting into acting, but what can you do when your self-appointed leader, Mark Constantine, discovers we have arrived on the same night as auditions for *The Importance of Being Earnest* and agrees to audition for the male lead?

While we waited in the green room to speak to the woman heading up the drama workshop, Mark was reading for the leading part of Mr Worthing, no doubt impressing the auditioning committee with his acting CV. These people were the theatrical cognoscenti who understood plays like *The Entertainer,* and Mark was cast for Mr Worthing. Talk about dramatic irony: to paraphrase Oscar Wilde, he 'had the misfortune to lose one parent' and, as he wasn't speaking to his mother, had been 'careless' enough to lose both. To be honest, I think they were desperate for a young male lead and Mark walked straight into the part, leaving his three companions slightly shocked. We had been looking for something to occupy us one evening a week maybe; now Mark was looking at a full-on rehearsal schedule and a week-long run.

1974, BOURNEMOUTH
Dressing up at the flat

When the committee found out that I possessed a tape recorder and a collection of BBC sound effects records, they said I could help with noises off. Mo and Geri were offered roles in the costume and scenery departments, which were housed in an old derelict church. The place was literally packed with period costumes, scenery flats, and furniture – everything you could possibly need to stage *War and Peace*. We had great fun borrowing the costumes for impromptu fancy-dress parties, something that became an annual ritual. Mark has never lost his boyhood love of dressing up.

Fortunately, after chatting to the leader of the drama workshop, Mark decided not to accept the invitation to play Mr Worthing, and soon our Wednesday evenings were taken up with improvisation and learning to act. This was fairly easy stuff for Mark and me as we had taken an evening drama class at Weymouth Technical College in the last year of our studies, but for Mo and Geri it was torture.

We had several months of rehearsals ahead of us for the first ever BLTC drama workshop. The idea was to present a series of short scenes from well-known and a few lesser-known plays on the theme of the seven deadly sins. Mo and Geri got speaking parts in an all-women scene from a Chekov play, and they were terrified. Mark landed a long monologue, which appealed to his poetic side, but I was given less demanding roles due to having to operate the tape recorder and cue in all the music and noises off.

Rehearsals for such an ambitious project were pretty intense and the commitment soon became more than just Wednesday evenings. Sunday afternoons appeared on the schedule, which was OK seeing as it was winter, but Mo was definitely not enjoying the acting, and Geri wasn't far behind her. With spring approaching, our producer gathered the cast together to inform us that we would be performing our show to the club members in a few weeks' time. It was very short notice and, as Mark and Mo had already planned one of their cycling weekends away in the New Forest on the same date, they refused to change their plans. A full-blown row broke out between Mark and the producer, with neither giving way, until Mark and Mo upped and walked out of the drama workshop, never to return. I've always wondered if Mo had been so scared of acting that Mark had deliberately engineered the situation in order to find a way out for her. Even to this day Mo is not overly comfortable with public speaking but she is in great demand as a leading British businesswoman.

Back at the flat, the theatre club was never mentioned again to the Constantines. Mark had left amateur dramatics behind forever and now held the transport brief in the local branch of Friends of the Earth. He and Mo had wanted environment but somebody had already taken that. Mark threw himself into the job with his usual zeal and soon he and Mo had pedalled their pink tandem around every street in Bournemouth and Poole, mapping out potential cycle routes. I would be drafted in to take photographs of key junctions and roundabouts for Mark's dossier and pinboard called 'Give Way', which he took to town-hall meetings and even made an appearance with it on BBC's *South Today*, our local evening news programme. I lent him my best tie so that he didn't come across as a tree-hugging hippie, which, in reality, he was.

Bournemouth had only recently been taken out of Hampshire as part of the Local Government Act 1972. The county line had cut through the conurbation at the edge of the borough at a place known locally as County Gates, although there wasn't a blade of grass between Bournemouth and Poole. The new Dorset boundary now extended to the eastern side of Christchurch. Bournemouth was a very affluent seaside resort, which considered itself superior to Poole, and the residents and council were generally not happy to be part of Dorset. The original plan was to link both Bournemouth and Poole to the A338 dual carriageway in stages. However, when the construction plans were unveiled, Bournemouth councillors were up in arms as large swathes of the town were earmarked to be bulldozed by Dorset Highways. With all this going on, the last thing anyone needed was some bloke from Friends of the Earth campaigning for cycle ways around the conurbation, although Mark was also against building the urban dual carriageway as it would decimate many acres of woodland.

When Mark gets passionate about something he is like a dog with a bone, and the campaigning lasted years, eventually evolving into a small action group called Transport 2000. Poole never did build the extension of the dual carriageway to connect it to Bourne-mouth and the east, although it does now have a great cycle-lane network, much better than Bournemouth. I'm not sure how much Mark and his colleagues influenced this, but he was in the vanguard of cycle lanes and an early anti-road-building activist – a view he still holds to this day.

As spring turned into summer, Mark and Mo spent more and more weekends with their friends John and Barbara who ran the youth hostel at Burley in the New Forest. John was a charismatic zoology graduate and one of the few people Mark has ever looked up to. He took Mark under his wing and gave him a free educa-tion in botany, teaching him how to recognise which fungi were edible and how to cook them, and the Latin names for plants and their culinary or medicinal purpose. John also introduced him to classical music.

At home, Mark would always have several botanical tomes on the go, not to mention textbooks on organic chemistry, which formed the essential basis of his ongoing trichology studies. At that time he was still only a preliminary qualified trichologist, and one day a week he worked on obtaining his intermediate certificate plus an advanced hairdressing qualification at Bournemouth Technical College.

With John as his mentor, Mark was making up for his wasted grammar-school education but he still had a massive hill to climb. He was only self-employed at the Poole salon and his income fluctuated from week to week. It was supplemented by him making shampoos, conditioners and treatments, which the salon bought from him at a very favourable price as they were supplying his workspace, plus consultancy fees for each head of hair he treated. If he made more than £25 a week he was doing well, but after paying his suppliers for the bases and ingredients that he used in his products, he was lucky to make £20. Mo was the principal breadwinner through her job as secretary to the Clerk of the Courts in Poole and her income was buying time for Mark to complete his studies and 'find himself.'

He was convinced there was money to be made out of selling herbal cosmetics but he couldn't work out quite how to do it. For the moment, he was intent on reading everything ever written about herbs and working towards a higher qualification in trichology. That would take him at least two years, so learning to live off the fruits of the forest became a way of life, and Mark and Mo experimented with all manner of organic foods, inspired by books like Richard Mabey's *Food for Free*, and even swapping bottles of herbal shampoo for flour at a local wholefood shop. Mo's bread- making skills were in their formative stage, veering from solid as a house brick to chewy, and what wine accompanies Lawyer's Wig stuffed with tomatoes or Elderflower fritters?

In the summer, Mark and Mo announced that they intended to cycle and hostel around the Brecon Beacons for their fortnight holiday. We saw them off on their tandem loaded down with bulging panniers, and reminded them to turn right

2012, POOLE
Publication of Mark's birding autobiography

out of the gate. I'm sure they had a map but I'm equally sure that Mark would not have planned the journey in much detail other than to avoid major roads. At what point they loaded their bike onto a train I don't know, but it was a seminal expedition. In his autobiographical book *Catching the Bug*, Mark describes this 1974 holiday in Wales as being the point where his interest in flora and fauna developed into a life-long passion for bird watching or 'birding', to apply the more commonly used term for the activity.

The hostel warden's garden was full of Pied Flycatchers, and he pointed them out to us from a shady seat. Eric must have liked us because he took us to visit a farmer's wife who had a couple of deserted cygnets on her pond. I remember him telling her, 'I hear the Reed Buntings are breeding again this year.' How intriguing. What sort of sound were they making? On the way back he suddenly hit the brakes and put the car in reverse to show us a Tawny Owl sitting in a bush on the side of the road. What wonderful birds! I was star struck with Eric's skill.

I wrote in the diary, 'He's the editor of *Breconshire Birds*, a National Park warden, a member of the mountain rescue team and it looks as if he's writing a book as well.' Silver Fern, bright blue bugs and Cuckoo Flower all dropped out of our notebooks and were replaced with Whinchats and Common Redstarts. In two hours Eric Bartlett had inspired Mo and me to become birders.

When he returned from Wales, Mark decided to get to know his 'patch', namely Poole Harbour and the surrounding areas, by immersing himself in local birding, and gradually he got to know everyone who was anyone in the Dorset birding community. He also added writing a book to his list of 'ways to make money' although he hadn't decided whether it would be about cycling or herbs.

Birding and campaigning for cycle lanes were largely daylight activities, and once winter set in again, it was back to playing games of *Risk* or a new battle game we had found called *Campaign*. Mark and Mo didn't own a TV and, as their flat was roomier than ours, we spent many evenings playing board games and listening to Mark's eclectic collection of records, which ranged from Cream, the Strawbs and the Zombies to classical and folk music. Mo was still trying to master the acoustic guitar and was a big fan of Joan Baez and Leonard Cohen. Geri and I were more into pop music, but in an attempt to broaden our taste Mark and Mo would drag us to a Bournemouth pub on a Sunday night to listen to folk singers like Vin Garbutt, who sounded to me like a guy singing with his finger in his ear. Who would have thought that forty years later, Mark would start his own record label, ECC Records, featuring many of the top folk singer-songwriters in the country, and that I would be the one raving about us all going to a free gig at a remote pub in the Purbecks, where Martha Tilston was playing.

One day, Mark came home with a flyer for a local war-gaming society, and the following Sunday we all went along to Pelhams community centre to watch a load of blokes fighting a Napoleonic battle with miniature model soldiers. Not just soldiers but cavalry, artillery, hedgerows and buildings, and even Wellington and Napoleon sat on their horses, commanding their armies. Mark and I were invited to command a regiment or two and we soon learned the rules of engagement. We were naturals! Our strategic skills, honed by years of playing endless games of *Risk* and *Campaign*, easily transferred to Napoleonic war-gaming – you just had to get superior forces into contact with weaker forces and battle it out with dice.

2018, POOLE

Mark's collection of Napoleonic strategy books

By that evening, Mark and I were hooked, and Mark was already planning which forces he would acquire for his British army. Oddly for a man who now often uses quotes from Napoleon's speeches to inform his thinking, he wanted to be Wellington, which only left me Bonaparte. But ahead of us were hours, days and weeks of painting model soldiers before we could even start to have a skirmish, let alone a full-blown battle.

Mark approached war-gaming in the same way that he approaches any subject that interests him: he focuses on it to the exclusion of anything else and batters it into submission. Mark found some seriously large books at the library, including *The Campaigns of Napoleon*, which stretched to several volumes. They were as thick as doorsteps, but we read them. Every time we fought a battle, Mark would surprise me with a new force of elite troops – Riflemen or the Rocket Troop of the Royal Horse Artillery. A few weeks later I would respond with a regiment of Polish Lancers or Chasseurs à Cheval. It also cost money, metal soldiers weren't cheap, but somehow Mark was outspending as well as outpainting me, no wonder they never had any savings. However, the time had come for us to combine forces.

Two guys from the war-gaming society had been keen to take us on for a while. They suggested a day's battle at their house in Ringwood, where they had a huge French army between them. Every war-gamer knows that you can refight the Battle of Waterloo a hundred times, and the French will always win. They should have won the actual battle, and at one point they had, but Napoleon, who was suffering from hemorrhoids on the day, didn't engage the Old Guard early enough. It stands to reason, therefore, that if you refight the battle with a model army, but don't make his mistakes, surely you must win?

To cut a long battle short, Mark and I applied every useful tactic that we had gleaned from Wellington's Spanish campaign. Mark's elite Riflemen created havoc, especially sharp shooting the French officers, and when you get it right, rockets fired into massed cavalry, causes mayhem. Just like the real battle, it was a close-run thing, but our better tactics won in the end and Mark could not stop talking about it for weeks. Years even!

Part of the reason why we had so much time on our hands was that our careers had slowed to a snail's pace. Mark had even taken careers advice and been told that none of the things he was interested in would ever provide him with a sustainable income. Just as well Mark ignored that advice or he might never have become the head of a billion-pound company. Mark was enraged by his employer's lack of vision for his herbal hairdressing products, but we had burned our bridges in London, and it was a time when being employed was a whole lot better than being unemployed. Our wives' incomes meant that we could afford a nice flat and, in Mark and Mo's case, buy a few luxuries like records, bird books and model soldiers.

By 1975 Mark had not yet formulated his future business plan, although he had met his future business partner. As well as having a resident trichologist, the Poole salon also had a resident beauty therapist, Elizabeth Weir. Liz was also self-employed, and was dating an Iranian Engineering student who coincidentally rented the flat above ours and below Mark and Mo's. Mark and Liz had plenty of downtime between clients and so began to talk about the future of hair and beauty products and how that future was going to be 'green.'

I was also looking for pastures green. My filmmaking activities had now become subsumed into general advertising and promotional work and I was often shipped off to trade exhibitions up and down the country. Also my travels around the declining industrial heartlands of Great Britain were broadening my horizon and I was determined to find a way out of my dead-end job, even if that meant giving up filmmaking.

Eventually I found an advertisement in *The Stage* for a job as an assistant manager at a community theatre in Whitehaven, which even came with its own council house. I applied for the job and was invited for an interview. Mark took it upon himself to prepare me. The internet had not been invented but he had a copy of *The AA Guide to Great Britain*, and so we discovered, for example, that Whitehaven hosted the world gurning championships, where people attempt to pull the ugliest or most comical faces, and that nearby St Bees Head was the site of Britain's highest lighthouse. Questions like these formed the basis of mock interviews that Mark conducted in the days leading up to the actual interview. It's a very long train ride from Bournemouth to Whitehaven via Barrow-in-Furness, and back again. Let's just say that knowing the height of St Bee's Head lighthouse didn't get me very far, but Mark will still check my memory - it's 335 feet, including the cliff it's perched upon!

Despite the effort he had put into coaching me, Mark seemed quite pleased that I would be staying in Bournemouth, and not long afterwards I found a new job a in a Boscombe graphics studio that specialised in the design and photography of wallpaper room-sets and catalogues. The company was owned by Clive Holmes, a man who would play a big part in the design of the iconic Cosmetics To Go mail-order catalogues in years to come. I was given my own production office and a studio full of brand-new photographic equipment to play with including my dream camera, the Hasselblad 500 CM, which now has pride of place in my collection of cameras. Mark was still studying for his intermediate trichology qualification, still spending as much time as possible learning about plants and birds, and still searching for an idea that would allow him to make a living out of his expanding but highly esoteric knowledge of hair and herbs. He was also the driving force behind our latest joint venture: we were now all signed up for organic gardening. The TV sitcom *The Good Life* was at the height of its popularity and it was the only time of the week that Mark and Mo would come downstairs to watch our TV.

They were already trying to live an alternative lifestyle, but living in a third-floor flat with no garden left only the wilderness as a source of free, natural food. What we needed, according to Mark, was an allotment, which he had duly applied for and had been granted. It was a few miles away, behind a council housing estate in north Bournemouth, and so we all drove out in my newly acquired Vauxhall Viva to visit 'our' plot. It hadn't been in use for years and was essentially just a large area of grass with the remnants of a compost bin at one end. Mark informed us that we would have to 'double-dig' the ground with spades and feed it with compost. For this, he already had a plan to collect fruit and veg waste from local greengrocers. 'In what?' I enquired. The thought of driving around Bournemouth, collecting sacks of rotting vegetables in my nice saloon car was not appealing, nor very practical, I argued. Coming from a long line of agricultural labourers I didn't need to watch *The Good Life* to know that we required manure, and tons of it. Fortunately, one of my work contacts owned a riding school with his daughter and had an endless supply of manure. I gave him a lot of business, so in return he was happy to deliver all the manure we needed to the allotment. Unfortunately, he could only just get his trailer inside the allotment gate and no further, so we devoted a long weekend to ferrying it through to our plot in a borrowed wheelbarrow.

As summer turned into autumn we spent our free evenings double-digging the rock-hard allotment with spades. I say 'we' but I can't remember Mark turning a single sod of earth; instead he did lots of measuring, standing on the manure heap issuing orders, and occasionally relieving himself upon it, telling us that urine 'would help break down the manure.' We all had our own views on what we should

1976, BOURNEMOUTH

Geri on our shared allotment

grow. I was a dyed-in-the-wool potatoes man; Mo wanted soft fruit; Geri favoured green vegetables; while Mark wanted herbs, of course. He drew a map of the plot and allocated the areas like a Napoleonic battle plan, convincing us that, come the following spring and summer, we would have masses of organic food for free. What we got, however, was the driest summer on record and a hosepipe ban!

# <u>07</u> Anita

1976 was a pivotal year in all our lives, but the most significant event for Mark, in terms of what followed, happened in Brighton. On Saturday 27th March Anita Roddick opened her first Body Shop.

In her biography *Body and Soul*, Anita Roddick describes how she founded the business by selling skincare products based on the ways indigenous women from remote areas of the world had been using organic lotions and potions for centuries. She had discovered many of these in her travels around Polynesia. Anita described these native women as having 'natural beauty' and 'smooth, soft and elastic skin' without ever coming near any of the overpriced and over-hyped glamour products of the mainstream cosmetics industry. She saw a gap in the market for 'natural' cosmetics, which would appeal to women like herself, people who were tuning in to an alternative lifestyle, although she never expected it to become a global brand.

Her husband, Gordon, told her she would need to take at least £300 a week and, if it wasn't working in six months, to give it up. Everything was handmade, even the now-famous logo cost only £25 to design, while the labels on the bottles were handwritten in ink, which often ran in steamy bathrooms. Anita started with just a handful of products, sourced from various small suppliers as she was not a cosmetic chemist herself, and claimed the shop looked like 'a country store in a Spaghetti Western.' Pretty much all the things she did by necessity, in order to keep costs down, became the founding principles of The Body Shop, but – like any new retail outlet – her first year was a tough one.

Back in Bournemouth, Mark was totally oblivious to the fact that sixty miles along the coast, the answer to the problem he had been trying so hard to resolve – how to make money out of herbal hair and beauty products – had just been solved. Or that the woman who cracked this nut would change his life in such a profound way.

Far from being aware of this hugely significant development, Mark was now embroiled in a battle with our landlord, who was attempting to sell our flats to make way for a private hospital development. Mark and Mo had enjoyed their light and airy 'penthouse flat' for over three years. It was brand new when they moved there in 1973, so to be given just three months' notice to leave was quite a shock.

After years of saving hard, Geri and I had taken out a mortgage on a spacious ground-floor flat in Talbot Woods, several months before the leaving deadline. Mark and Mo were only a ten-minute walk away but, where we now had our own home and a stable joint income, they were still in limbo, hamstrung by the slow progress of Mark's career and quickly becoming the only tenants of a soon-to-be-demolished block of flats.

It's never a good idea to make Mark angry, because he will fight to the bitter end against anything he believes is unfair. His favourite quotation is from a Thomas Jefferson speech: 'In matters of style, swim with the current. In matters of principle, stand like a rock.'

As one of the few businessmen to take on Amazon and win, he knows how to push people's buttons. In 2014, when the giant online retailer refused to stop using the word 'lush' as a means to direct customers to Lush-like products, Mark sued for breach of trademark, as Lush does not sell online through Amazon. Amazon fought the action and lost, but decided to up the ante and lodged an appeal. Mark responded by registering the name of the UK CEO of Amazon, Christopher North, as a trademark and duly created a shower cream called 'Christopher North' – 'a shower smoothie, rich, thick and full of it' according to the description on the label. He then promised to launch it in his shops if Amazon did not back down. The point Mark was making was that Lush was a trademark that Amazon was not legally allowed to use, whereas 'Christopher North' was now a trademark that Lush was legally entitled to use. Mark had trademarked his own name, just to be on the safe side, but Amazon backed down and the appeal was settled, an outcome that in my view should have prompted David Cameron to recommend Mark for a knighthood, to highlight a successful British business standing up to a powerful corporate bully.

In 1976, though, Mark was locked in battle with his landlord, and reckoned that he was entitled to at least six months' notice, knowing full well that a sitting tenant would seriously impede the sale of the property. Having a wife who worked for a lawyer gave him some extra leverage too. He managed to push the landlord to the point where he actually paid Mark to leave, which gave them enough money for a deposit on the modest semi-detached house in Poole that they moved into that April. 174 Rossmore Road was not in a 'des res' location. For a start, it wasn't anywhere near Poole town centre but perched on a hill in the outer suburbs, in an area of dense mixed housing. The £6,900 price tag was the maximum they could afford, but at least it was downhill all the way to work on their bikes.

I hired a van to move them across town as, despite having lived in a furnished flat, Mark and Mo owned a large double bed that had been a wedding present from Mo's parents. They had acquired enough belongings to fill two or three van trips but their new home was seriously short of furniture. Downstairs was a front-to-back lounge/dining room leading to a small kitchen and an even smaller bathroom. Upstairs there were two bedrooms and a box room, which

Mark had earmarked for his laboratory. It was quite a small house, but they did have a shed for their bicycles and a back garden. Also, a near neighbour called Dave Collins was a prolific beekeeper, with a local stock of honey and beeswax, staple ingredients of natural cosmetics. Mark discovered several racing pigeon enthusiasts living a few streets away and organised an endless supply of pigeon shit for our allotment. Let's just say we managed only one big load, and this time I insisted that Mark did his fair share of shovelling shit into plastic sacks. It took forever to clean the boot of the car and purge the smell, and from then on Mark ferried his rotting fruit and veg to the allotment on his bike.

We were now four years on from the original master plan to get out of Weymouth and head to London. It had seemed like an eternity but Mark, the eldest, was still only twenty-four, and Geri, the youngest, just twenty-one and mistress of her own home. Although I had turned my back on industrial filmmaking, I did have a stable and very creative job as a studio manager and photographer. I was even involved in a slow-burning film project with a deaf graphic artist, Jill Mansfield, which would reignite my passion for film-making and lead to a groundbreaking film about deafness called *I'm Only Deaf.* We shot the film in Mark and Mo's house during one of their nature watching weekends in the New Forest, although they weren't too pleased to see us still there at midnight on the Sunday.

The next year was all about fixing up our new homes and trying to grow our own fruit and vegetables in the middle of a drought. Technically, being a resident of Poole, Mark

2018, POOLE

Mark's first home at 174 Rossmore Road

was not allowed to rent an allotment in Bournemouth, so we just swapped the address to our flat and kept Mark as the named tenant. Geri was doing most of the gardening anyway; she had acquired a bike and regularly rode to the allotment after work with a hoe tied to the frame.

Despite never being one for physical work like digging and hoeing, Mark had nevertheless built a laboratory at home in his box room, with a bench, a large Baby Burco water boiler and a collection of pots and pans. Laboratoire Garnier it wasn't, and some of the concoctions in his plastic containers were the colour of mud – one of them might even have been mud – but he was making progress.

In the summer of 1976 Mark passed his intermediate exams in trichology and was writing articles and a book for the Herbal Society, having befriended the father of modern herbalism, Dr. Malcolm Stuart. The book was about herbal hair colours and detailed all the herbs that historically have been used for hair dyes. The queen of natural hair dyes was henna, a herb found in North Africa, the Middle East and on the Indian subcontinent. Mark was always telling us that the synthetic hair dyes being sold by the big brands were known to have carcinogenic qualities, whereas henna was a completely natural material that coated the hair rather than pene-trating it. There was red henna for brown or auburn hair, and black henna for black hair, but there was not one for blondes, although Mark was developing something with camomile. Today, he is prob-ably one of the world's foremost authorities on henna in terms of its use in cosmetics, but back in 1976 he was still trying to make money from all these strands of knowledge.

As a last resort, Mark decided to leave the hairdressing salon and set up a cosmetics manufacturing business in the box room at his house. He was tired of trying to convince his employers of the merits of herbal hair products, especially as they were always more interested in the product name rather than the efficacious nature of the contents. For example, when Mark invented a rosemary and nettle shampoo, they came back and said, 'very good, but let's call it sage and yarrow.' The fact that the shampoo didn't contain sage or yarrow didn't matter; it sounded better than something with nettles in it and would therefore be easier to sell to the customer. Despite these disagreements, the salon was still happy to buy hairdressing products from Mark, and even gave him some business advice: 'Buy the raw materials, sell it for double what you paid, reinvest it, and don't let your wife get hold of the money.'

M. Constantine Cosmetic Manufacture, wasn't a limited company, just a trading name, and it didn't have many customers. I remember Mark cooking up quite a big order of elderberry shampoo for a local chain of herbalists. It was the colour of claret when I delivered it for him, but a completely different colour a few weeks later when I collected it again from the shop. The whole batch had gone off, and so began a lifetime's work for Mark in the field of natural cosmetic preservatives.

While Mark beavered away in his lab, Anita Roddick's first Body Shop in Brighton had grown through blood, sweat and tears into a reasonably sustainable business, so much so that she was convinced she needed to open a second shop. As she said herself in her biography *Body and Soul*, 'Entrepreneurs are doers as well as dreamers – they want to find the best way to push an idea along and use money to oil the wheels.' But finding the money to open a second shop was not so easy and, with Gordon away crossing South America on horseback, she made a huge business decision without him. Her friend Aidre, who was going to manage the new shop in Chichester, told Anita that her boyfriend Ian McGlinn, would provide Anita with £4,000 in exchange for a 22 per cent stake in the business. Famously, Anita thought it was a good deal and wrote to Gordon, who was adamant that she should not do it. However, by the time his letter arrived from South America, Anita had already sold a large chunk of The Body

Shop to a local garage owner who had some spare cash. When The Body Shop went public in 1984 his stake was worth £4 million and ultimately it rose to over £140 million

The Chichester Body Shop opened in September 1976 and was based on the same model as the Brighton shop. By Christmas, both shops reached the milestone of making £100 each on the same day. They still had a limited product line but they were catching the attention of the press, including a small article in *Honey* magazine, which was aimed at teenagers and 'gay get-ahead' young women. Mark first heard about Anita in this *Honey* article and decided to contact her, as she recalls in her own book:

Early in 1977 I got a telephone call from a young herbalist called Mark Constantine. He had written a book about herbal cosmetics and was trying without a lot of success, to market his own herbal shampoos. He wanted to know if The Body Shop would be interested. I remember that he was calling from a payphone and had to keep feeding coins into it. I was having trouble finding cocoa butter at the time and I asked him if he made anything that used it. He said he did - his uncle worked at a chocolate factory and could get all the cocoa butter he needed. I was keen to extend our range of products, so I asked him to come and see me at the Chichester shop.

Mark turned out to be as manic a herbalist as I was a trader. He was tall, dark, a kind of hippy character, and we hit it off immediately. He was studying trichology at night and spending his days dreaming up wonderful herbal products that he could not sell because they looked so bloody awful. He made a henna cream shampoo, for example, that looked like sludge and smelled like horseshit, and a honey and beeswax cleanser with black specks caused by bees returning to their hives with dirty feet. I thought we could overcome the problem with cards explaining what the products contained and why they looked the way they did, so I swallowed hard and gave him an order worth £1,000. It was a record for both of us - the biggest order I had ever placed and the biggest, by far, that he had ever received.[1]

[1] Body and Soul, Anita Roddick 1991

1991, BODY & SOUL

Signed copy of Anita Roddick's autobiography

That was an understatement; Mark came home from Chichester in a state of euphoria and terror. He told us that the moment he walked into The Body Shop he knew he had found what he was looking for, and he was blown away by Anita Roddick whom he saw as a complete visionary. However, the massive order that she had placed with him was terrifying, because he did not have the money to make it and Anita was probably breaking the bank to buy it. It was going to have to be cash on delivery because his suppliers would only extend him thirty days of credit, and he had a lot of product to make in his box-room manufacturing plant. And where was he going to store it? If this lot went off there would be no coming back.

Naturally, being the only driver, I was drafted in to deliver the order and so for £18, I hired the biggest van I was allowed to drive. I remember pulling up at his house in Rossmore Road and Mark opening the front door to show me what we had to load. The house was full of five-litre plastic containers of shampoo and whatever else he had made. They were everywhere: in the lounge, the back bedroom, the bathroom, and even up both sides of the staircase, leaving just a small gap down the middle.

We covered the entire floor area of the van with gallons of product. I don't know how much it weighed but I was worried about stacking it too high in case one fast bend sent the whole lot flying. The cab only had two seats, so Mo and Geri had to be wedged in the back of the van between the containers before being shut in for the two-hour drive to Littlehampton. We organised a form of Morse code for communication. Two bangs and everything was OK, three if we needed to stop.

Anita didn't have room to store Mark's bulk product at the shop so we were delivering it to her house to be stored in the garage, which she used as a bottling plant. As it was a Saturday she was working in the shop in Brighton, leaving Gordon to take delivery. God knows what he must have thought when we opened up the back of the van to reveal our wives surrounded by a ton of shampoo but, after offloading the order, we all sat around the Roddicks' kitchen table drinking tea while Gordon wrote Mark a very large cheque. It was actually for £1,572.75; the entry was recorded in Mark's first ledger and it was by far the biggest one up to that date.

Goods delivered, we drove from Littlehampton to Chichester, where Mark treated us all to fish and chips and a tour of The Body Shop. It was like a country store from a western, with bunches of dried flowers hanging everywhere and shelves full of the iconic Body Shop bottles with their handwritten labels. Anita said the new products all sold out within a month and so she placed an even bigger repeat order with Mark. I put him in touch with a proper deliveryman that I knew, and so began a very fruitful relationship between Mark and Tony 'Van', as he became known.

We didn't need to be told when a Body Shop order was in production at Rossmore Road, as a trip to the loo would reveal stacks of finished product occupying every inch of spare space. The box-room lab was above the kitchen and one day Mark melted a plastic dustbin with a mixture of beeswax and almond oil that was too hot. It came through the ceiling and coagulated around the light fitting. The resultant brown stain was there for years.

Almost as soon as the first Body Shop cheque was safely cashed in the bank Mark opened phase two of his business. Working from home, there was only so much he could do in terms of product development. Asking friends and family what they thought of his latest product wasn't overly scientific, but at least it didn't involve the barbaric practice of subjecting defenceless animals to laboratory tests. He still needed the hands-on feedback that only comes from using your own products on lots of different heads of hair. So, late in 1977, Mark rented three rooms in a former pub at 29 High Street in Poole with his new business partner Liz Weir, the beauty therapist he had worked with at the salon in Poole. They called themselves the Herbal Hair and Beauty Clinic and they offered trichology and beauty treatments using natural cosmetics, which of course they made themselves. They branded their limited range as Constantine & Weir's Country Cosmetics, which Liz touted around local markets and speaking engagements at Women's Institutes. Mark and Liz even made up a song about them: 'Constantine & Weir's Country Cosmetics – good for your health and good for your hair.'

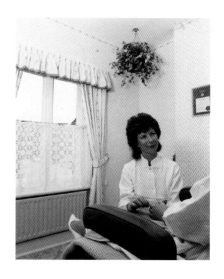

1977, THE HERBAL HAIR AND BEAUTY CLINIC
Liz working in the beauty therapy room

The Herbal Hair and Beauty Clinic was on the first floor of 29 High Street and consisted of a reception-come-consultation room, a beauty therapy room and a trichology room, the latter fitted with infrared lamps that looked like something out of a science-fiction thriller. It needed publicity photographs, of course, which I took, and not for the first time Geri volunteered to have her hair hennaed. We also roped in Paul Lawley, one of the hairdressers from Mark's former salon to do the styling and to bring in a few more willing models who didn't get paid but instead got a free haircut and a new hair colour.

CONSTANTINE
&
WEIRS'
COUNTRY
COSMETICS

1977, 29 HIGH STREET, POOLE
Constantine & Weir' Country Cosmetics label

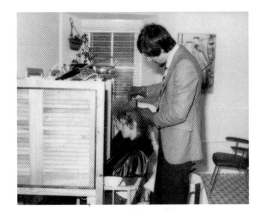

Mark at work in his Marigolds

This was the first of count-less shoots I have done at 29 High Street down the years. To this day, it remains the heart of the business, where the founders have their labs above the Lush shop and spa. They now own the whole building and the one next door, but whenever I go in there I can still picture Mark standing in his check jacket, flares and Marigold rubber gloves, slapping green goo on a woman's head and wrapping it in cling film. I know the process so well that I can henna my wife's hair.

The Herbal Hair and Beauty Clinic only survived thanks to the inexorable growth of The Body Shop, which ensured that Mark had a constant stream of income from the manufacturing side of the business. Gordon Roddick had the brilliant idea of franchising the business, so that anyone who had enough money and the right attitude could open a Body Shop in their own town. The smart ones like Deb McCormick, a young economics graduate, opened half a dozen outlets, starting in Bath in 1978.

Anita, Deb and Mark formed a very close troika, bouncing ideas off each other to grow the product range, much of which was developed and tested at the Herbal Hair and Beauty Clinic before being mass-pro-duced in the box-room laboratory at Mark's house, including some of the early products like henna shampoo, Elizabethan washballs

Red Geri

and elderberry conditioner.

As well as running his clinic by day and manufacturing by night, Mark was also holding short courses for Body Shop staff to teach them about the products and how to advise customers on skin and hair care. He has a famous talk entitled 'Birth of a Spot', which he still gives to his own staff today. It was recently turned into an animated film and dubbed in a dozen languages. Back in 1978 it was done with a flipchart and a magic marker, but there's no

1977, THE HERBAL HAIR AND BEAUTY CLINIC
The trichology room

doubt that the customer service for which The Body Shop was once renowned was heavily influenced by Mark's input. He and Anita understood that product knowledge was the unique selling point of the natural cosmetics business, so staff training was always a top priority – as it is in Lush to this day. Indeed, Lush regularly comes out top for customer service in high-street surveys.

Looking back, it's hard to imagine that Mark and Mo managed to meet the demands of the early years of the Body Shop's growth, from 1977 to 1981, entirely from their little semi-detached house in Poole. There was no time for Napoleonic war-gaming now – or very much else, for that matter. The allotment was now almost entirely the preserve of Geri, who was rapidly becoming a convert to self-sufficiency. Although Mark and Mo had sown the seeds of 'food for free', they were too busy servicing The Body Shop to help with growing fruit and vegetables. In fact, Mo had given up her job in the law courts to become a full-time cosmetics manufacturer.

One day in 1979 I returned home from a business trip to find my wife terribly excited. She had found a run-down smallhold-

1980, THE BODY SHOP

Herbal Hair colours range invented by Mark

ing of almost an acre of land in a village just outside Bournemouth and wanted to buy it. It included a converted dance hall, an orchard and even a flock of egg laying ducks! We sank every last penny into the purchase of what became our family home, and as money was going to be tight, Mark suggested Geri become his first outworker, bagging henna for The Body Shop. Liz would turn up in her car every couple of weeks with drums of powdered henna, which Geri had to weigh into plastic bags, neatly fold, seal and place into pre-printed cardboard sleeves. Keen to contribute actual money to our family income and help pay the mortgage, which had soared to a 13 per cent interest rate, Geri bagged henna in the evenings wearing marigolds and a very uncomfortable breathing mask. By the end of the evening she was covered in fine green dust, except for the clean patch around her mouth and nose.

With The Body Shop now opening stores in other countries as well as all over the UK, Mark and Mo were gradually making enough money to build up some serious savings, although if you ever visited their house at Rossmore Road you would never have guessed it. After an amateur attempt by Mark to knock out the old chimney, he banned himself from DIY for evermore on the grounds that he might actually kill someone. They had managed to decorate the lounge/dining room in a light country style, including painting the floorboards bright green, which served as a sort of oasis in a house otherwise dedicated to making Body Shop products. Mark and Mo had also expanded the Herbal Hair and Beauty Clinic, taking on a new reception room, which they almost completely filled with a large green leather-topped desk. I took a publicity photograph of Liz sitting behind the desk looking like Miss Moneypenny.

1980, 29 HIGH STREET, POOLE

'M will see you now'

The clinic was the hub of the R&D side of Constantine & Weir. Dozens of women and a few men were regularly sent products to test or came into the clinic for trials and henna parties. With such a love for nature and the environment, Mark was never going to go down the path followed by mainstream cosmetics manufacturers and test his products on animals. It was also the stated policy of The Body Shop that they were Against Animal Testing, and Mark played a big part in shaping that policy, with Constantine & Weir becoming one of the first cosmetic manufacturers to develop an alternative test to dropping liquid cosmetics into rabbits' eyes. The Assisi Project, as it became known, was still a few years away at this point but it helps to explain why Lush now puts up a £250,000 Lush Prize every year for scientists working in the field of alternatives to animal testing. It stems from the very core of the business and principles that were laid down at the birth of the small company that eventually became Lush. To date, Lush has awarded over £1.8 million to the most effective projects and to the individuals who have been working towards the goal of replacing animals in product or ingredient safety-testing across five strategic areas: Lobbying, Public Awareness, Science, Training and the Young Researcher awards.

Although Mark and Mo were busy building their business, we still shared a joint hobby thanks to Dave the beekeeper and, as a big user of honey and beeswax, Mark was naturally keen to learn all he

2015, LONDON

Lush Ethics Director, Hilary Jones, presenting
an award at The Lush Prize

could about the art of beekeeping. Dave had dozens of beehives and he would take Mark to the various locations where he kept his bees, each site carefully selected on the basis of the plants that flowered there; near lime trees for lime-flavoured honey; in heather for a rich dark-brown honey; and amongst dandelions for a very light, yellowy honey.

This was all grist to the mill in Mark's never-ending search for new product ideas, so he decided to become a beekeeper. As we owned a large garden and plenty of fruit trees in need of pollination, he suggested that Geri and I did the same. So we all became members of the East Dorset Beekeeping Association. Mark opted for a couple of beehives in his garden shed, while we went for the more tradi-tional garden beehives with the little house roof. Dave taught us all about it: how to catch swarms and introduce them to an empty hive; how to open the hives every nine days to check for signs of swarming; when to take off the honey and, most impor-

1980, LONGHAM, DORSET
Dave and Mark with my first beehive

tantly, how to do it without getting badly stung. Dave would regale us with great stories of beekeeping disasters and offered brilliant tips like: 'When you hear the bees sounding like Spitfire engines, close them up as quick as you can.' This advice was to prove invaluable in the not-too-distant future.

In the early summer of 1981, Geri and I turned up at Rossmore Road and were shocked to discover that Mo had cut off all her hair. Mo had always had long, straight hair down to her waist, now it just about covered her ears. That wasn't the only change, though. After much nodding and winking, we discovered that Mo was pregnant and the baby was due in December.

Production for The Body Shop hadn't slowed; in fact it had exploded thanks to Mark inventing Peppermint Foot Lotion, which was initially part of a PR stunt to coincide with the first London Marathon. The Body Shop's PR consultant Janis Raven had the brilliant idea of getting Body Shop staff to massage the feet of the runners after they finished the race, and tasked Mark to come up with a suitable product. The resulting publicity ensured Peppermint Foot Lotion became one of the biggest-selling Body Shop products of all time.

Rossmore Road was bursting at the seams, and with a baby on the way an expansion of the business was urgently required. Most people would have opted for a small factory unit but, typical of Mark, he bought a large Arts and Crafts house, in a des-res suburb of Poole with views across the harbour. It boasted so many rooms that you could get lost on a tour of the house, and a large tiered garden with steps leading down from a patio to a lawn and then into woodland. It also had a large shed-come-garage that has gone down in Lush folklore as Mo's lab where the bath bomb was invented, plus an air-raid shelter in the front garden, which might come in handy if Ronald Reagan succeeded in starting a nuclear war.

Mark had plenty of help from Tony Van to move everything from Rossmore Road to his new home, with the exception of the two beehives in the garden shed. Moving them required expert help, but Dave was away for a few days. We had been beekeeping for several years now, and Mark had gradually become more familiar with his bees, just wearing his veil on warm summer days when the bees were happily popping in and out of the holes in his shed wall, loaded up with pollen and nectar. Now it was autumn, when the bees were all at home, which is what we wanted, however it was a bit overcast, which Dave had always told us, was not the ideal weather for working with bees. The plan was to lay a white sheet in front of the hive entrance and then lift each hive out of the shed and onto the sheet in turn. Then after any stray bees had gone back inside, wrap the sheet around the hive so that no bees could escape, before carrying it to my car. 'Simples!'

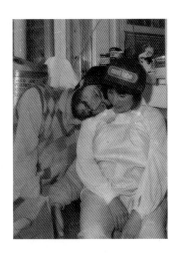

Mark and Mo in the Pudding Club

It was warm enough for Mark to be wearing light clothes and red All Star Converse trainers – plus his beekeeping hat and veil, of course, as no one likes being stung on their face. I was more cautious on the other hand and dressed in the full suit with integral hood and facemask plus gloves and boots. As always, a few bees were coming and going so we waited for dusk, when Mark sealed off the entrance with a strip of wood. The house had already been sold and the new owners were watching the proceedings from the kitchen window with Mo and Geri. Mark and I were both in the shed now, ready to lift the first hive.

The hives had been in position for a couple of years and, unknown to us, the bees had formed a propolis seal with the wooden floor. 'One, two, three – lift!' The hive only partly came away from the floor, and whatever Mark used to seal the hive entrance fell out. A few bees emerged at first, quickly followed by a lot more, and then the Spitfire engines fired up. You couldn't count the number of times Mark got stung in the few seconds it took him to carry the hive to the sheet, and even then hundreds of them chased him up the drive past the startled onlookers. I just stood still in a dark corner of the garden, safe inside my impenetrable suit as the bees dive-bombed my defences. The beehives did not get moved that night, and we waited for Dave to come back the following day and show us how to do it properly, which took him all of five minutes!

Moving house did not just give Mark a larger space in which to make cosmetics, it also prompted a call from his half-sister Laura when the change-of-address card came through the post at the

family home that Mark had been kicked out of when he was seventeen. Mark had not seen Laura or his mother since his wedding in 1973, eight years earlier. Now approaching sixteen years of age, Laura decided to contact her big brother, and he agreed to meet her off the train at Poole station. Not many teenage sisters get picked up on a tandem and are asked to pedal harder, but that was Laura's first encounter with her estranged half-brother who was fifteen years her senior and now sported a black beard. I thought he was doing his best to

1981, POOLE
Laura making tea at Mark's house

terrify her, but Laura stayed at the new house with Mark and Mo for a week in the school holidays and she was soon a regular visitor, even donning a white boiler suit and working part-time in the home factory. It didn't lead to an immediate reconciliation between Mark and his mother, although it eventually came about thanks to Laura's persistence.

On 22nd December 1981 Simon Constantine came into the world and more photographs were taken for the family archive, and on Christmas Day Geri and I drove over to the new house to cook Christmas lunch. Most of the rooms were still largely empty as Mark and Mo owned very little furniture, but there was a roaring log fire in the red-brick fireplace in the lounge, where we ate and celebrated with the Christmas bundle of joy. By the time we had finished the washing-up, Mark, Mo and baby Simon were fast asleep, so we slipped out of the house and left them to their dreams.

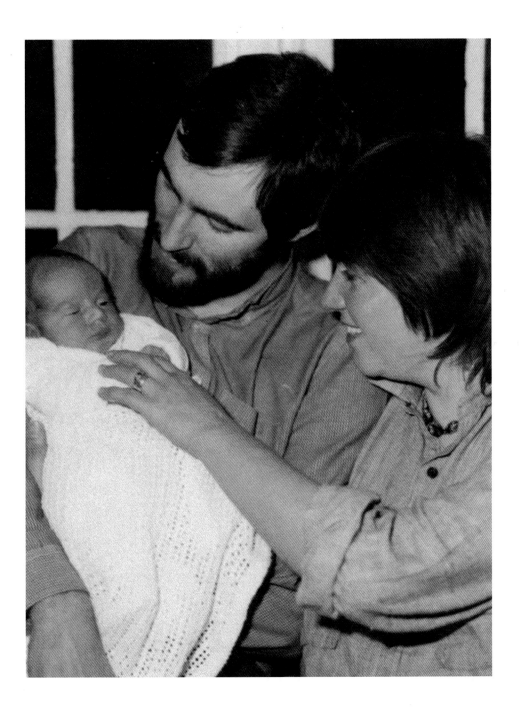

1981, POOLE

Proud parents and baby Simon at Christmas

# <u>08</u> Aunty June

Mark was now a father with his own son to cradle, just as his father had cradled him a year before disappearing into Africa in 1954. Dear John had no idea that he had just become a grandfather, and great-grandmother Matilda Constantine, who was still alive and living in Manchester in 1981, was none the wiser either.

These were the thoughts that were going through my mind in May 2012 as I read and re-read Matilda Constantine's death certificate. What an unlucky lady she was to lose contact with both her son and her grandson, and never to know that she was a great-grandmother. Why did Mark never think to look for his grandparents? Why did his mother never tell him where they lived? Perhaps he thought they had died when he was younger, just like his maternal grandparents.

At least Matilda had her daughter June to comfort her and, thanks to the information on June Constantine's 1963 marriage certificate, I was confident that I would find her living in Manchester. I couldn't explain the lack of a birth registration but I now knew she was born in 1945, so she was only seven years older than Mark. Twenty-four years had passed since the death of Mark's grandmother, but I searched in the obvious place first: the Constantine family home of many generations in Little Hulton. Sure enough, June Howarth and her husband Richard were listed at that address on the electoral roll for 2012. I now had proof that the sister of Mark's father was alive, and a quick search on 192.com gave me her telephone number.

It was approaching the end of May 2012 and I had a decision to make. June Howarth née Constantine would almost certainly know something about the whereabouts of Mark's father, but equally she must have known about Mark and yet the family had seemingly never tried to find him. By now, you could simply Google the name Mark Constantine and find countless articles online about his business, his politics and the OBEs that Mark and Mo had recently received for services to the cosmetics industry.

I decided to write to June, explaining that I was an amateur genealogist researching the Hyde Constantine family history. I didn't mention Mark, or John, in case it was a sensitive family subject. I needn't have worried; on the Queen's Diamond Jubilee bank-holiday Saturday, while I was sitting on a boat in Portland Harbour, June phoned my mobile and immediately started telling me about her family history. She confirmed that John Constantine was her brother, and without a pause for breath she added that he had a son called Mark who lived in Weymouth. What an irony; here I was in Portland, looking out over Wyke Regis where Mark lived with his grandmother until he was twelve, talking to a lady who not only remembered him as a baby, but who had actually stayed with Mark and his mother for one summer holiday in 1952. And Mark didn't know she even existed.

With her broad Mancunian accent, June sounded like a character out of *Coronation Street*, and I warmed to her immediately. Then a sudden thought hit me. Maybe June didn't fully know her own family history; perhaps the reason why I couldn't find her birth record was because she had been adopted. I certainly didn't want to be the person to tell a sixty-seven-year-old lady that she wasn't who she thought she was, when she had so kindly responded to my letter. I made an excuse about not having my research notes with me, which was true, and promised to call her back a few days later.

On the Monday I sailed back to Poole in a squall; rain, hail, waves breaking over the bow, normally conditions that would dampen your spirits. One of the crew was seasick in his bunk, the cooker broke loose and fell onto the floor of the galley with an almighty crash, and the tiller extension broke off in my hand during a tack. It was a wild ride but I couldn't have been happier. I had found Mark's long-lost aunty, the sister of John Constantine, and I was sure there was a lot more to come.

As soon as I got home I looked again for June's birth certificate. I had her exact date of birth but my search was still coming up with a blank. I called her on the Tuesday night and pretended that I didn't know her precise birth details 'Oh, you won't find my birth certificate,' she replied. 'I were adopted but they didn't tell me until I was twelve. I gave them bloody hell as a teenager.'

It was at this point that I came clean with June and told her that I was Mark's best friend from childhood and that I was compiling his family tree and if possible trying to locate his father in time for his sixtieth birthday in July. She told me that they had also lost contact with John in the early 1980s and that her mother had died broken-hearted. June was as interested in finding out what had happened to her brother as Mark was in finding his father, and so we made a pact to work together and maintain secrecy until Mark's birthday.

June remembered that she had stayed with Mark and his parents in Kingston during the summer of 1952 while her own mother was recuperating from an illness, and that Mark and his mother had visited the family home before John left for Kenya. After that they hardly saw John, except when he returned from Kenya following a lung illness in the late 1950s and again when he remarried in 1964. Until I found June I had been a lone detective trying to work out the puzzle, now I had 'Miss Marple' on my side and the clues flowed thick and fast. June told me I was only the second person to come looking for her brother; a man had turned up in 1963 needing to contact John in order for Diane to file for a divorce. That could only have been Eric, Mark's stepfather – more evidence of how much information had been kept from Mark.

June was now able to tell me the story of how her brother John had remarried after the divorce and that he and his new wife, Prudence, had two daughters while living in a village near Dursley in Gloucestershire. She gave me one exact birth date and one approximate date. A few days later I had found the birth records of Mark's half-sisters and was soon in possession of copies of their birth certificates. These told me that from 1966 to 1969 their father was working as a health-physics monitor at the Berkeley nuclear power station on the River Severn. Joanna Constantine, the elder daughter, was born in December 1966 and Sarie, the younger, in July 1968. Laura, Mark's maternal half-sister was born in 1967, so now he had three half-sisters, all of a similar age.

In the space of a week I had added an aunt, an uncle, two sisters and two cousins to Mark's family tree. I quizzed June about John's job and she told me he had emigrated to South Africa to work in the nuclear industry in 1969 but that she didn't know whereabouts. She thought it might be Durban.

I searched the records of the Union-Castle shipping line, as it was the main passenger carrier between Britain and South Africa at that time. I eventually found John Constantine, his wife and their two infant daughters on the passenger list of the SA Oranje, which sailed from Southampton to Capetown on 3rd January 1969. John had a one-way ticket to start a new life in South Africa, completely unaware that his sixteen-year-old son Mark was wasting his education, was at war with his stepfather, and was in desperate need of some contact with his birth father.

June told me that her parents travelled from Manchester to Southampton Docks to wave goodbye to their only son, unaware that they would never see him or their granddaughters again. They

| UNION-CASTLE LINE | | | | | | | OFFER OF ACCOMMODATION | | | | |
|---|---|---|---|---|---|---|---|---|---|---|---|
| Ref.: P/ 3 Date 9/10/68 | | FORWARD VOYAGE | | | | | RETURN VOYAGE | | | | |
| This offer will be held until 31/10/68 Reservation beyond that date is conditional upon payment of the fare or a deposit of not less than 20% | Ship | " S.A.ORANJE " | | | | | " | | " | | |
| | Sailing Date | 3-1-69 | | | | | | | | | |
| CLASS OF TRAVEL | FORWARD T. | RETURN | From | UK | | | | | | | |
| | | | To | CAPETOWN | | | | | | | |
| NAME(S) OF PASSENGER(S) | | Berth | Grade | £ | s. | d. | Berth | Grade | £ | s. | d. |
| MR. J. CONSTANTINE | | 3 berth | T4 | 37 | — | | | | | | |
| Mrs — " — | | outer Cabin | | 37 | — | | | | | | |
| Mill. — , — (2) | | plus COT | | 345 | — | | | | | | |
| Miss — " — (infant) | | guaranteed | 13 | 14 | — | | | | | | |
| AGENT OR PRIVATE ADDRESS | | Single Ticket Basis* | 321 | 9 | — | | Single Ticket Basis* | | | | |
| S.A. Agency Office | | Return Ticket Basis* | | | | | Return Ticket Basis* | | | | |
| Chichester House. | | 10% rebate | 32 | 3 | 10 | | | | | | |
| 278 High Holborn | | Current Net Fare | 289 | 5 | 2 | | Current Net Fare | | | | |
| W.C.1. (Miss Dodson | | Delete if inapplicable | | | | | | | | | |
| The accommodation offered is in a ........... berth ........... cabin | | Immigrant fares are quoted subject to confirmation from the South African Embassy. | | | | | | Total | | | |
| McC. 1694. | | | | | | | | Please Turn Over | | | |

John Constantine's one way ticket to South Africa

too had no knowledge of the life of their grandson, who at that precise moment in time was just forty-two miles away in Weymouth. 'Why didn't they try to contact him?' I enquired. June said the family presumed Mark had taken his stepfather's surname, and that so much time had passed that it would have been unfair to suddenly upset that relationship.

From my conversations with June it was clear that Mark's paternal grandparents were very conservative people from a working-class mining and cotton-making community. Maybe love and loyalty for their son overrode any desire to make contact with their grandson, knowing that to do so might jeopardise the new life John was about to make with his second wife and family.

I now had a similar problem. A quick way to find John Constantine might be to try to contact his daughters on Facebook, even though they were probably married and had changed their names.

Mark as a baby in his mother's arms

But what if they had never been told they had a brother, or indeed that their father had abandoned his first wife and child? That news could upset the relationship with their parents if they were still alive. Some people don't want to be found.

The missing pieces of the puzzle arrived in the post a few days later. It was a parcel from June containing photographs from her mother's box of memories, which had been stored in a bag in the loft at the family house in Little Hulton since Matilda died in 1988. I was trembling with anticipation when I removed the first photograph from one of several envelopes. On the back in blue ink was written the date, 21st July 1959, Mark's birthday. I turned it over and choked back the tears as I stared at the picture of a seven-year-old boy proudly wearing his new primary-school uniform.

This was the Holy Grail that I had been searching for – family photographs. There was only one way that Mark's paternal grandmother could have a picture of her seven-year-old grandson: Mark's mother must have sent it to her. In addition, there were other photographs of Mark at a younger age – not many, but enough to show that Diane had kept some contact with her mother-in-law until it was clear that her marriage to John was over.

There were more photographs: Mark as a baby with his mother and father, his parents' wedding day, a wartime photograph of his

1950, WYKE REGIS, WEYMOUTH

The wedding of Mark's parents

<u>LEFT</u> Mark's great-grandmother, Margaret Bridge
<u>RIGHT</u> John Constantine with baby Sarie 1968 <u>BOTTOM LEFT</u> Mark's grandparents at Southampton Docks
January 1969 <u>BOTTOM RIGHT</u> Joanna and Sarie growing up in South Africa

grandfather, the wedding of Mark's paternal grandparents in 1927, even a picture of his great-grandmother on his grandmother's side of the family. It was like opening a treasure chest. Other envelopes contained photographs of John with his baby daughters in Gloucestershire and on the beach with their grandparents, photographs of them leaving at Southampton Docks, and many more photographs of the two girls, Joanna and Sarie, growing up in South Africa.

The last photograph showed Mark's half-sisters with their mother, Prudence, and the family dog. I figured the elder girl looked about fifteen and so I dated the picture to around 1982. They were taken at a new house on a plot of land that overlooked a panoramic view of the countryside and some very large industrial buildings in the distance. I studied the thirty-year-old colour photograph for ages. This was it, the home of John Constantine, the long-lost father of my best friend. But where in South Africa was it?

# <u>09</u> Team Building

January 1982 saw unemployment in the UK reach a post-war record of 3,070,621, and mortgage interest rates were an eye-watering 15 per cent. Mark and Mo had paid £52,000 for their large house in Poole, including £10,000 in ready cash that they had saved in the five years they had been supplying The Body Shop. Neither the Constantines nor the Roddicks were yet making huge fortunes from the steady growth of The Body Shop, which was now opening shops at a rate of two a month.

It was still strange to walk into a rambling Arts and Crafts house in the midst of a leafy suburb to find the back kitchen and utility room converted into a small cosmetics factory. To us it felt like Mark and Mo were desecrating a lovely old building. It was even stranger to find a couple of school-leavers in white boiler suits, stirring vats of whatever was being made to fulfil the next Body Shop order – quite how they found their way to the newly constituted Constantine & Weir Ltd was difficult to fathom. Yet, slowly but surely, Mark was gathering together a bunch of part-timers and odd-job people, many of whom, like Julie Panton, would stay loyal to the company forever.

We happened to be visiting one day in April when a smart young woman came to the door for an interview with Mark. Her name was Helen Ambrosen, and she had first come across the company as a client of Liz at the clinic. Helen was seeking a herbal remedy instead of a conventional steroid cream for her eczema, and Liz recommended her a honey beeswax and jojoba cleanser.

When Mark advertised for someone with a science background to help make products, Helen saw her dream job. A former researcher for the Institute of Terrestrial Ecology with a good knowledge of botany and chemistry, she already understood the benefits of natural ingredients and how to synthesise formulae. Goodness knows what she thought of the small factory in the old

1984, CONSTANTINE & WEIR LTD

Helen Ambrosen

kitchen or the lab in the garden shed, but in joining Constantine & Weir she made the best career decision of her life.

Helen is one of the founders of Lush, and since 1982 she has provided much of the science behind the thousands of products invented by the company, including the solid henna bar. If you have ever tried using powdered henna and mixing it into a paste, you will understand how much easier it is to melt a chunk of solid henna. Helen is the patent holder of solid henna as well as many other Lush products, and is famous for her Ultrabland cleanser. Shortly after joining the company, she brought in a tall, gangly twenty-year-old called Karl Bygrave and trained him to make products. Karl is now a director of Lush and has been responsible for a lot of the overseas development of the company, including setting up Lush Japan, although that was sixteen years in the future.

1984, CONSTANTINE & WEIR LTD

Karl Bygrave

As well as the home factory, which was pretty much dedicated to making Body

Shop products, the Herbal Hair and Beauty Clinic was continuing to grow and take on staff. While much of its remit was testing new products to sell to The Body Shop and other smaller customers, the clinic still offered day-to-day trichology and beauty treatments to the public. Earlier that year Mark had engaged another young woman who would help drive the business forward: Rowena Hofbauer, a newly qualified beauty therapist with a passion for make-up and no end of ideas for developing colour cosmetics. A vivacious blonde with a smile made in Hollywood, there was no way Mark wasn't going to employ Rowena, even if he didn't have a specific job for her. Whereas Mo, Liz and Helen were the quiet women who went on to found Cosmetics To Go and Lush, Rowena was more flamboyant, constantly changing her hair colour, make-up and wardrobe, sometimes in outrageous ways.

1984, CONSTANTINE & WEIR LTD
Rowena Bird (née Hofbauer)

She had the personality to host her own TV show and in a few years time she did.

One day in late summer, Clive Holmes Studios, where I was now a director, received the news that the Shand Kydd wallpaper factory in Christchurch was closing. Almost overnight we lost 60 per cent of our business, and with it the company's planned expansion into corporate video services. I am by nature a cautious person and, unlike Mark, not prone to spur-of-the-moment decisions, but when Clive told me we'd have to tighten our belts and drop the video plan, I reacted by telling him that I would go it alone and set up my own business.

When I discussed my plan with Mark, his initial reaction was to offer me a job as his production manager. The Body Shop was opening a warehouse in Littlehampton and product was flying out of

Mark's home factory as fast as he could make it. I think he thought I'd made a reckless decision and he was just throwing me a lifeline, but there was no way I was ever going to work directly for Mark. Being close friends with someone is a lot different to working side by side with them, and I knew sooner or later it would result in conflict. Instead, with the help of his accountant, Mark showed me how to write a business plan and, thanks to Margaret Thatcher encouraging banks to back new business ventures, I secured a three-year business start-up loan for £10,000 and a £3,000 overdraft that I had to secure myself. On 1st January 1983 I became managing director of my own photography and video production company and immediately started losing money.

The Body Shop's overseas expansion was growing even faster than in the UK, and Mark spent a lot of time travelling with Anita Roddick. On a trip to Sweden, they found that the Swedish franchisee had sub-franchised into Finland, where someone had put their own twee interpretation on the classic Body Shop design. Mark said Anita went ballistic, as she did with anyone who deviated from the Body Shop concept. Little did Mark know that one day he too would be on the receiving end of Anita's wrath.

1985, CHRISTMAS PARTY
Mark & Mo with Anita & Gordon Roddick

In the early 1980s The Body Shop was still a small private company with a turnover of less than £750,000, but it was great fun for everyone involved. Mark and Mo spent a lot of time in the company of Gordon and Anita, and one Christmas Mark rewarded his major customer with daily gifts to mark the twelve days of Christmas. Tony Van delivered livestock including three hens and six live geese to Gordon and

Anita's house, while on day nine, a ladies Morris side danced through the Roddick's warehouse waving their ribbons and handkerchiefs. It wasn't all one-way traffic though. I remember Mark telling me that on one occasion he had got into an argument over the phone with Anita about something he had done wrong for which she had called him 'unprofessional'. He told her 'you can call me anything you like, but you cannot call me unprofessional'. A few hours later a grinning deliveryman arrived at his house with a bouquet of flowers and a gift card with just one word on it - 'wanker'.

In September 1983, Mark and Mo announced they were expecting a second baby in June of the following year. Simon was now twenty-one months old and running around the home factory while his mother and her team made cosmetics. Even Karl was changing his nappies – in between producing batches of henna cream shampoo, which had a remarkably similar constituency.

Then in October, the four of us headed to London to take part in the biggest CND rally ever to shake the city. Ronald Reagan and Margaret Thatcher – fresh from her landslide election victory in June – were ratcheting up the cold-war tension with the Soviet Union. American Pershing cruise missiles were now being based in the UK and other countries in Europe to face up to the Soviet Union's SS20 missiles being deployed along its European borders. It was all pretty serious stuff, with cruise missiles being moved around the countryside at night on transporters, which is why a group of women decided to blockade the gates of the US Air Force base at Greenham Common and set up a peace camp there.

Mark and I were inspired to join CND when the government started issuing the civil defence publications *Protect and Survive.* The leaflets informed you what to do in the event of a nuclear attack and how to survive it, which of course was complete bullshit. So, over the Easter weekend of 1983, we had joined the CND rally to link arms across a fourteen-mile route from the Aldermaston atomic weap-

ons research centre to Greenham Common. At the end of the day
the police herded us into a holding area for our coaches and forced
us to wait there until way after midnight. We lit bonfires to keep
warm, using anything that would burn, and strangely we seemed
to be as unwelcome with the women's peace camp as we were with
the police.

Undeterred, and with Mo back in the family way, we took the
train to London on 22nd October to march from Westminster to
Hyde Park. It was during this rally that I took a black-and-white
picture of Mark in his beret, looking every inch like Che Guevara.
We also ended up in a national newspaper picture, standing under
the banner of the Cambridge Anarchists. I think Mark has been on
a police watch list ever since.

1983, LONDON

Mark looking like Che Guevara on the CND march in October

The following April, The Body Shop was floated on the stock exchange. Starting at a price of 95p, it settled at £1.65 a share. With thirty-eight Body Shops to supply in the UK and fifty-two overseas, there was much coming and going from Mark's home factory – too much for one neighbour. One day, when Mark returned home from watching the UK release of *Return of the Jedi*, a man from the planning department was there to greet him. It was a fair cop, Mark knew he was breaking planning regulations, but he liked working from home. However, the business was now turning over £500,000 a year and he could well afford a small factory unit.

Liz found some space to rent in an old lighting factory on Sterte Road overlooking Holes Bay in Poole Harbour, so Mark only had to cross the road to go birding. The move took place in the final months of Mo's pregnancy, and on 11th June 1984 Jack Constantine was born. Not everything was moved to the factory unit – the green garden shed was left kitted out so that Mo could still work from home while bringing up two boys.

In August, our own little bundle of joy, John, came along. We had survived a difficult first year of our start-up business enterprise and extended our mortgage by ten years to pay for it, but Constantine & Weir were finally spending some of that Body Shop income with me. It was just a few short training clips at first. Mark had invented banana conditioner, which involved his staff peeling hundreds of bananas that were then mulched into an oily liquid. Mark had got the idea from a story he heard of a Land Rover breaking down in the jungle due to a dry gearbox. The driver had chopped down some bananas and, using the mashed fruit as a substitute for gearbox oil, he was able to lubricate the cogs and drive to safety. I don't know whether it was a true story, but Mark wanted to turn it into a video – a very cheap one, of course. As luck would have it, a botanical greenhouse in our home town of Weymouth had recently made the news for growing a giant bunch of bananas. I persuaded a man from the council to let me film it, and then smuggled Mark in, complete with pith helmet, to recount the story for the benefit of Body Shop employees. A few days later, some vandals broke into the greenhouse and stole the bananas.

1984, 29 HIGH STREET POOLE

Opening party

Despite a steady stream of income from The Body Shop, Mark's bank was constantly telling him to diversify and not put all his eggs in one basket. He had always supplied a few small customers like herbalists and hairdressing salons, including Michael John and John Frieda, and every so often he would invest in people or a business that might provide additional streams of income. The Herbal Hair and Beauty Clinic occupied only the first floor of 29 High Street, so when Paul Lawley, a hairdresser from the same Poole salon that had employed Mark and Liz, set up his own small salon and took space on the ground floor, it was inevitable that Mark would branch out into hairdressing.

1984, 29 HIGH STREET POOLE

Paul Lawley

The building already provided trichology and beauty treatments and it made sense to add hairdressing as well. Mark acquired all the ground-floor rooms and used money from his manufacturing business to give the building a makeover and provide space for an R&D laboratory.

The factory unit was also expanding and taking on staff, so there was quite a gathering of people at the opening party of Paul Lawley at 29, which took place in the reception area of what became the first

Lush shop and is now the Poole Lush Spa.

In the first year of public ownership The Body Shop added fifty new shops and profits soared to £2.4 million. Servicing this growth was a nice problem to have, and fortunately for Mark the factory in Poole had plenty of space into which it could expand. Nothing went out in five-litre plastic bottles anymore, it was giant sixty-litre blue barrels of the stuff and liquid pallet containers. People kept joining the company both at the manufacturing end of the business and on the R&D side where Mark was building up a stable of experts in perfumery, botany and cosmetic chemistry.

Foremost among these was Stanislaw ('Stan') Krysztal, a respected London cosmetic chemist who had worked on leading brands including Mary Quant and Nivea. He was already in his seventies when he started working with Mark and his colleagues, and his experience was to prove invaluable. Stan's belief that inventing cosmetics was more of an art than a science would become a philosophy that underpinned the creation of Cosmetics To Go and which the Lush founders still employ to this day. A Polish refugee fleeing Nazi Europe when he first came to Britain in the 1930s, Stan was proud of his Polish heritage. Stan died in 1992, but Mark told me that he would have been overjoyed to see so many of his countrymen working for Lush today, and the company's stance on freedom of movement.

Other experts on the payroll, in one form or another, included Jeff Brown, a perfumer who supplied the fragrances for Constantine & Weir, and Dr Malcolm Stuart, a renowned botanist and herbalist who was a larger-than-life character in every way. When these specialists

1985, CONSTANTINE & WEIR LTD

Stan Krysztal

all gathered around Mark and Mo's
dining table, anything was possible.
Mo actually invented the prototype
of the bath bomb during the course of
one of these meetings, popping backwards and forwards from her lab in
the shed. On another occasion I found
a man in a white lab coat, Stephen
Smalls, working in Mo's shed. He had
already invented a new product called
hair gel - it was clear and smelled of
coconuts. Stephen, who was one of

1985, CONSTANTINE & WEIR LTD

Dr. Malcolm Stuart, Jeff Brown and
Stan Krysztal

Mark's trichology contemporaries, explained that the problem he
had to solve was how to preserve it, and he gave me a pot to test,
although I wouldn't have been seen dead with gelled hair.

It was now 1985 and my two-year-old video production business
was still returning only just enough income to live on, and often I'd
have to wait months before I could pay myself. To grow my business, I needed a large customer who required videos on a regular
basis, and unsurprisingly I couldn't identify many in Dorset. If only
I could get a customer like The Body Shop. That was it, the answer
was staring me straight in the face. With fifty shops a year being
added to the business and Mark chasing all over the place training
Body Shop staff, a regular staff-training video for The Body Shop
was the obvious way to go. I pitched my idea to Mark and he agreed
to set up a meeting for me with Gordon. Even if I say it myself, I
wrote a really good presentation for Body Shop TV, right down to
how the monthly VHS tapes would be distributed and viewed. Each
shop would rent a TV and VHS player from Radio Rentals, just like
people did at home. The programme itself would be a mixture of
news, training and special documentary features, and it would all
be pulled together once a month with a one-day shoot presented by

Anita herself. I had seen her talk to her staff and it was a no-brainer.

Gordon thought it was a great idea, and I felt confident about the project until Anita's people at Body Shop HQ informed me that Body Shop TV was going to be put out to a three-way competitive pitch, but naturally I would be one of the three. I already had quite a bit of footage of Body Shop products being made at Constantine & Weir, plus a few of Mark's training clips, so all I really needed was a few hours in Body Shop's flagship shop in Great Marlborough Street with Anita. This would be my unique selling point, so it was disappointing when Anita's PA informed me that Anita would not be presenting Body Shop TV – ever.

I should have ignored those instructions and hired an Anita Roddick lookalike actress. Instead, I took a more conventional approach and lost the pitch to a company who went on to become a major London corporate video production company, largely on the back of Body Shop TV. In the years to come it was painful to watch the regular Body Shop communications videos called *Talking Shop*, an interesting mix of news and documentary features presented by... Anita Roddick.

Mark was equally disappointed and immediately said that we could at least produce training videos for the major products that he supplied to The Body Shop, starting with the new hair gel. He gave me carte blanche to come up with an original idea and, for a change, a decent budget. The result was *Twenty Things to do to with Hair Gel* where the hero, a private detective, has to solve the theft of twenty boxes of hair gel by tracking down the culprits by their hairstyle. It was the best script I had written to date, delivered in the first person by the detective's own voiceover. It was a spoof of the classic American detective genre and was full of witty one-liners. I did have to find twenty cheap models or actors but, with a full team of hairdressers and beauticians at 29 High Street to call on, hair and make-up was essentially free.

Mark loved the script and even suggested that when we did the big reveal at the end – that it was the detective himself who stole the final case of hair gel – we should get Gordon to play the slick gumshoe and wink at his staff. But then he had another great idea (as is often the way with Mark: take the possible and make it impossible or at least extremely difficult). Paul had suggested bringing in a top London stylist to help with the hair, someone really in vogue in the West End.

OK, that sounded all right if Mark was prepared to pay his huge fee. But why not go one better and make a behind-the-scenes video: *The making of Twenty Things to do with Hair Gel* featuring the hairdressers talking to camera as they worked on the models' hair. 'But Mark that will be longer than the main video, a lot longer!'

Naturally, as Mark was paying for it, I had to shoot the 'making of' video, side by side with the main film, but it was hugely ambitious and the scheduling was a nightmare. One scene required four models dressed as femmes fatales to be filmed having their hair done, with running commentary from the two stylists, and then we had to whip them across the road to a bar that had only given us permission to shoot for a couple of hours. Despite cutting a few corners to come in on budget, I turned in two films that met Mark's approval, and Gordon did play the final shot of the slick-haired detective to perfection, right down to the knowing wink. However, I was never convinced that an entertaining ten-minute spoof required a forty-minute behind-the-scenes video to accompany it. But it was the first big production that Mark had commissioned from my company – and he really made me work for it.

1985, POOLE

*Twenty Things to do with Hair Gel* video

The following year we made another training film for The Body Shop called *A What's On Guide to Herbal Hair Colours*, which featured four young women sharing a house and learning to colour their hair with The Body Shop's range of herbal hair colours, manufactured by Mark (and bagged by Geri). It was shot as a thirty-minute sitcom in the style of *The Liver Birds*, and we built a lounge and kitchen room set in my studio. It had a very authentic 1980s sitcom feel and featured young trainee actors from the Bristol Old Vic Drama School. Once again, Gordon made his cameo appearance at the end of the film.

1986, CONSTANTINE & WEIR LTD
Steve 'all things to everyone' Brackstone

Throughout this period, Mark's cosmetic manufacturing business was expanding rapidly to keep pace with The Body Shop. Hair Gel had become a bestselling product, and the factory was now making it by the ton. When you entered the main compounding area there was a line of four massive stainless-steel mixing vessels and boiler-suited compounders wheeling barrels of ingredients around. One of these was sixteen-year-old Steve Brackstone, a lad who joined the company straight from school and is now such a Lush legend that he became known as Steve 'all things to everyone' Brackstone. He even went on to become the first co-presenter of Lush TV.

In 1986 Anita was named Businesswoman of the Year. Mark suggested that The Body Shop share price would go up when this news was announced. In fact, it went down, but that was not a problem as Mark had already embarked on a cunning plan to expand his business. The experts he had gathered around him had by now started generating so many new product ideas and formulae that The Body Shop could not accommodate them all in their range.

I even produced a corporate video for Constantine & Weir called *The Original Cosmetic Company* so that they could market their products elsewhere. Retail was the way to go, but Mark could not compete with The Body Shop as they were his biggest customer. Except in one part of the world.

When Anita opened her first Body Shop, it was inspired by a visit she had made in 1970 to a herbal cosmetic shop in Berkeley, California, owned and run by two sisters-in-law, Peggy Short and Jane Saunders - it was also called The Body Shop. I doubt that Anita ever thought her Body Shop would become a global phenomenon, but when it did, she could not operate in the USA because she didn't own the trade name. The Body Shop name was registered to the two women in California.

Enter Mark Constantine. For some years now Mark had been visiting North America, often combining this with visits to Mo's sister Jane, who was now married and living in Seattle just over the border from Vancouver, a city that would ultimately be home to the HQ of Lush North America. Although there was always a birding element to his travels, Mark was also visiting every hippie-inspired cosmetics outlet on the West Coast, looking for ideas to diversify his business.

In Pike Street Market, one of the oldest farmers' markets in the USA, situated on the waterfront in Seattle, Mark met a woman called Faith Weinberg who sold cleansers and cakes of soap from a basement shop called The Cleansing Bar. Talking to Faith gave Mark an idea for opening a Body Shop-type store in a suburb of Seattle and he came up with the name Bodkins. In Mark's mind, Bodkins was the perfect way to get around the The Body Shop's trademark issue, and – with a sister and brother-in-law, Barry, willing to work for him – he could open a small US retail business quite legitimately. So far so good.

1986, SEATTLE, USA
The Bodkins range

Starting with not one shop but two - one of them in the Medical
Dental building in downtown Seattle and the other in a specialist
retail village in Issaquah on the east side of the city – the venture
seemed a bit optimistic. This was highlighted when I asked Barry
to send me some video footage of the stores for viewing at the
annual Constantine & Weir company day. I had already filmed short
features of Mark's various business arms – a botanical plant grower

in Cambridge, a trichology clinic in Wimbledon, the new R&D set-up and testing centre in Poole – so all I required to complete the presentation was a video report on the progress of Bodkins. Rowena was presenting the show for me from the sofa at 29 High Street, having dipped her toes into live TV when promoting a Bodkins makeover on a Seattle cable TV channel.

It was deemed a bit expensive to send me to Seattle, so Barry shot the Bodkins video report himself on a camcorder. Instead of just sending pictures, he did a sort of fly-on-the-wall documentary with running commentary. It included footage of his garage and basement bursting with Bodkins product, but not in a good way, and footage of the stores, which were largely devoid of activity until we heard Barry say 'Oh look, a customer!' as if one only came along every hour, which wasn't far from the truth. I showed the footage to Mark before heavily editing it to make Bodkins appear more businesslike, and Rowena provided a scripted commentary. The shops still looked devoid of customers, which was a bad sign, and there was more trouble just around the corner.

It's hard to remember which bombshell landed first. I knew that The Body Shop was building their own global HQ, factory and warehouse in Littlehampton, and that Gordon and Anita had asked Mark more than once to become their head of R&D, but that would have meant closing his Poole business. However, he did agree to *pretend* to be their head of R&D when Princess Diana opened the new headquarters in December 1986. I'm sure the opportunity of meeting the Princess was more of a draw for Mark than putting on a white lab coat for Anita, and I know he was very nervous about doing it. If he did it too well he would risk upstaging Anita, but if it went badly he would get the blame. Unsurprisingly, the TV cameras majored on Mark and Princess Diana sharing a joke about the facemask he was making. A short-lived moment in the limelight, as Anita was on the point of finding out about Bodkins.

HRH Princess Diana and Mark at the opening of The Body Shop
factory in December

Mark and Gordon spent a lot of time in each other's company, and Mark told me he often had to watch what he was saying or signing if he had drunk too much wine. Despite this, he insists that he was upfront and straight with Gordon about his US retail adventure and they had agreed that, if things went well, Bodkins could be The Body Shop's way into the US market.

Telling Gordon was one thing but telling Anita was another, and when she found out about Bodkins, from Gordon, it was carnage. Mark used to do a great impersonation of Gordon: 'F... fucking hell Mark, she nearly killed me!' Mark and Gordon's gentlemen's arrangement, whether it was made at the end of a bottle or not, wasn't going to be tolerated by Anita. After investing £200,000 in a business that was probably going to fail anyway, Mark pulled the plug on Bodkins.

In between all this, our second son, Michael, came along so we had levelled the score at 2-2 with the Constantines. However, having failed to find any large scale clients for my start-up business in three years, I had given up my studio, slashed my overheads and was now working mainly as a freelance director for larger corporate video production companies and advertising agencies. I even had an ACTT union card, writer/director, a mere 15 years after I first applied.

The Bodkins affair had soured relations between Mark and Anita but Constantine & Weir were still trying to diversify the business away from one all-consuming large client. In their sights was the mail-order clothing company Banana Republic. Mark was a big fan of both their clothing and the style of their catalogue, which contained lots of airbrushed illustrations and travel stories, so back in the lab Rowena, alongside colleagues Stephen Smalls and Sue Sievers, hatched a plan to develop a range of travel cosmetics to pitch to them. It was all pretty secret – so secret that even Mark was kept in the dark, and I heard about it only after the event. Unbeknown

Rowena's Africa Wrap which sparked the start of CTG

to Rowena and Stephen, however, Banana Republic was already in talks with The Gap about a possible takeover and never responded to their speculative pitch.

Undeterred, Rowena boxed up her hessian wrap containing a range of travel cosmetics, and sent it to Mark while he was attending a Body Shop conference. Despite having previously told Rowena to drop the idea, he loved the appeal of mail-order cosmetics for two very good reasons; Constantine & Weir were now developing products faster than The Body Shop could take them, and The Body Shop could not open a mail-order business as it would compete with their own franchisees.

Here was the opportunity to diversify without stepping on the toes of The Body Shop, and so it came about that Constantine & Weir gave birth to Cosmetics To Go. Rowena's range of travel cosmetics, later known as African Companion, sparked a revolution in mail-order cosmetics that would have far-reaching effects. The first catalogue was launched in February 1988, echoing but not copying the style of the Banana Republic catalogues. A few months later The Body Shop opened in the USA after it had purchased the trading name from two sisters in San Francisco for $3.5 million.

Having turned down some of Mark's more unusual cosmetic products – like the bath bomb, which Mo had invented as a gentler alternative to bath salts, and the solid shampoo bar, which pretty much lasted forever – The Body Shop was now embarking on a manufacturing revolution of their own. It's hard to understand why The Body Shop did not simply offer to buy Constantine & Weir, rebrand the factories in Poole and make Mark a director of the company. He was Anita's natural successor, had invented many of their bestselling products and had been influential in shaping their ethical and environmental policies. Instead, they all reached a deal whereby The Body Shop would buy the manufacturing rights to all their products produced by Constantine & Weir, for an agreed sum of £9 million to be paid in three £3-million tranches. In return, Mark agreed not to open a rival retail high-street cosmetics business for three years. In the meantime, he would continue to supply The Body Shop until their new factory was fully operational.

1988, POOLE
The first Cosmetics To Go catalogue

Mark accepted the deal, knowing that he could plough the money straight into Cosmetics To Go and keep his factories running and his staff employed, which now numbered over a hundred people. The new mail-order business – with its innovative products, colourful parcels and free post and packaging – was, in the words of the

*BBC Clothes Show* presenter Jeff Banks, 'bringing fun to bath time all over Britain.' TV was going to play a big part in the public awareness of Cosmetics To Go, and in the late summer of 1988 Mark gave me the brief of my life: he instructed me to come up with a publicity film for Cosmetics To Go – and I could spend up to £50,000.

**THE STORY OF THE COMPANY THAT CAME BEFORE LUSH**

# DANGER
## Cosmetics To Go

A cosmetics company
on the edge!

by Mira Manga

# <u>10</u> Danger! Cosmetics To Go

To fully appreciate the whirlwind story of Cosmetics To Go you need to read Mira Manga's book, *Danger Cosmetics To Go*. It's a kaleidoscope of the stories, products and people who all embarked on a five-year journey into the unknown. Or, to borrow the *Star Trek* split infinitive, 'to boldly go where no other cosmetics company had gone before.'

Without a doubt, the stand-out product of the first mail-order catalogue was the African Companion range of travel cosmetics. It didn't require too much brainpower on my part to work out that a documentary of an African travel adventure would make the ideal subject for a publicity film. But where? A journey across the Sahara to Timbuktu; tracking the source of the Nile to Victoria Falls; or how about unravelling the exotic mysteries of Zanzibar? For someone who hadn't been further than the French Riviera on a camping holiday, the pages of the African travel brochures that I devoured in the late summer of 1988 appealed to the Boy Scout in me like nothing had ever done before. I turned a page and found myself staring at a large bull elephant standing in a glade of acacia trees and, towering above it all, Mount Kilimanjaro with its white snow-topped cone glinting in the African sun. The photograph was taken in Arusha National Park in Tanzania and it immediately gave me an idea: Cosmetics To Go did not test its products on animals but it did test them on humans, so why not send some humans to a land of animals, and test them on a journey from the wild plains of Africa to the freezing snows of Kilimanjaro, and make a film about it?

I pitched the idea to Mark, saying we would have to find a couple of fit CTG customers to be the subjects of the film as there was quite a lot of serious uphill walking involved – not least, a thirty-six-mile trek from 6,000 feet above sea level to over 19,000 feet, where the air is very thin and the chance of succumbing to altitude sickness is quite high.

Mark loved the idea and, as luck would have it, in addition to the African Companion travel wrap, CTG had recently developed a selection of cold-weather lip and skin balms called Below Zero, aimed at skiers and travellers to cold places. Mark's PR guru Janis Raven – the same person who had masterminded Body Shop's public relations and was now contracted to do the same for Cosmetics To Go – suggested one of our two travellers should be a cosmetics journalist in order to maximise press publicity, and she proposed Susannah Kenton, daughter of Leslie Kenton, the former editor of *Harpers & Queen* magazine. Janis also advised that the other traveller should be Rowena as she had been the main architect of the African Companion range and so would be able to provide Susannah with all the product knowledge. Mark agreed with Janis completely. Susannah Kenton was an up-and-coming TV lifestyle presenter, and you only had to point a camera at Rowena and she would spring into life. It wasn't going to be a gritty *Everest the Hard Way* documentary, but a fun adventure of two young women taking on the highest mountain in Africa. I even had the title shot 'African Companions'.

The pre-production phase of the project was coming along nicely when I attended a regular meeting with Mark and Janis to update them on progress. As I walked into the room, I saw Mark holding a VHS tape in his hand and I could tell something scary was coming my way: 'Jeffrey, we want to make the first mail-order video catalogue.' By 'we' they meant me, and it needed to include a film or video about every product range in the CTG catalogue, not just African Companion and Below Zero, but also Sea Level, Gigaku, Baby Revels, Khufu and the rest. 'But Mark,' I protested, 'the video will be several hours long and how will anyone find the bit that they want to watch – keep winding the tape backwards and forwards?'

According to Mark that would be a minor inconvenience to the joyful CTG customers, most of whom would watch it from end to end and then lend it to their friends. The video would be free to anyone spending over a certain amount, or customers could purchase it. It was a bold but ridiculous idea; aside from not being able to find the start of each mini-film, every time a new product or range came out the video would be out of date. Today, non-linear digital formats like a menu-driven DVD or online TV channels make this sort of thing a piece of cake, but in 1989 you just had a 180-minute-long VHS tape with no search functions.

The project started to go wrong when Susannah's diary gave me only a ten-day window in February, the month we had to go for a chance of getting the best weather. The only schedule my fixer in Tanzania could arrange had us starting with a climb of Kilimanjaro, followed by a safari in the Ngorongoro game park. I had wanted to start in the game park, but we couldn't make the dates work. I told Rowena that the cold-weather products had better work as I needed them both to have the complexion of the classic English rose on day one of the finished film, although it would be day seven of our shoot.

Then, on the day of our departure, our flight to Addis Ababa was delayed by three hours and we missed our connection to Kilimanjaro International Airport. We were forced to take a flight via Rwanda and Uganda, arriving late at night to be greeted by

a baton-waving immigration officer who threatened to put us on
the first flight to Dares Salaam in the morning. So began the first
of many acts of bribery, which could have seen me thrown into a
Tanzanian prison at any time. It took $50 for me to convince the
immigration officer of our credentials and stamp our passports,
but only $25 for the customs officials, as they just asked for some
beer money.

God knows what time we arrived at the hotel near the gates of
Kilimanjaro National Park, but the next day our official mountain
guide Harold took one look at our equipment and demanded more
money for the porters and himself. He had us over a barrel as we
could not afford any delay in our timetable. If bribery was going
to be the way, I needed to get it on my terms so I took Harold to
one side and agreed to increase the porter's fees, plus a $100 bonus
for himself, on the condition
that he got us to the top of
the mountain.

1989, KILIMANJARO NATIONAL PARK, TANZANIA
Susannah and Rowena in their Safari outfits

We were the last party to
set out on the trail to the first
camp at 9,000 feet. Harold
and most of the porters had
gone ahead and left head
porter Charlie in charge, and
he beat out the rhythm of the
walk in Swahili, 'pole, pole'
(slowly, slowly).

An hour up the trail the heavens opened; rain fell in stair rods,
turning the dry red earth to rivers of mud. It was at this point that
Rowena and Susannah informed me that they had packed their
Gortex wet-weather gear in the sacks given to the porters, because
they thought it was going to be a nice day! So much for my pre-production instructions. The film crew all had ex-army cagoules but

Rowena and Susannah were in beige shirts and shorts and looking like drowned rats. After an hour of struggling to walk and film in the rain, we had to call a halt and just concentrate on getting ourselves to the huts without risking our equipment and film stock.

I don't actually remember arriving at the camp four hours later because apparently I fainted when the huts came into view. Harold, keen to earn his bonus, had run up the trail and bagged us two four-man alpine huts, which is where I woke up around dinnertime. The rain had stopped and the soaked safari outfits along with other trekkers' clothes were spread out to dry on the hot tin roof of the cookhouse. My cameraman, Derek Little, had continued filming in my absence and got some great shots of camp life and a brilliant rendering of the 'Jambo' (hello) song, which became our theme tune. The day and the altitude had taken its toll on me, but we were where we needed to be on day one.

The morning of day two saw Rowena and Susannah fully kitted out in their Gortex mountain kit, although in Susannah's case it was over her still slightly damp safari clothes. After a couple of hours of fairly steep trekking, we emerged from the rainforest onto open scrubland. The cone of Kilimanjaro was still two days away and was covered in cloud, as it was every day after 10am, so we had no view of our objective, only another six-hour walk to the next camp, situated at 15,000 feet.

After a couple of hours of stop–start walking, due to filming, it was clear that Susannah was struggling. As a vegan she had barely touched the camp food, nor

1989, KILIMANJARO, TANZANIA

Susannah and Rowena, Mawenzi in the background

had she taken any of the recommended travel immunisations. Now her Gortex jacket was sealing in the dampness from her clothes and she was shivering. I agreed to let her press on to the next camp with a porter, as we would be a lot slower with filming stops. By the time we reached camp two, Susannah was tucked up in bed, and by the morning she was turning blue from hypothermia. There was no alternative but to send her back down the mountain, courtesy of a stretcher mounted on a heavily sprung unicycle. We filmed the drama for several hours and consequently started the third day's trek up the mountain well behind schedule.

When we reached the plateau, at around 17,000 feet, the mist was so thick we couldn't see more than a few metres in front of us. Somewhere out there was the snow-capped cone of Kilimanjaro but we had yet to set eyes upon it. By mid-afternoon the mist had turned into a full-on snow blizzard and some of our porters had come out from the base camp at the foot of the cone to find us and help us in.

We collapsed into our bunks at around 7pm, knowing that at midnight we'd have to get up for the final 1,000-metre ascent of the snow cone. This was the point where I realised that I needed an extra day for the crew to recover, but we didn't have it in our schedule. At midnight we set off for the six-hour climb up the frozen snow, now in our alpine kit as the temperature was minus -15°C. We would not be able to film until sunrise at around 5am so, provided we kept a steady pace, we should make it. Only an hour into the ascent Rowena announced that she couldn't go any further, then over the next two hours, my PA Suzi and Caroline the sound record-ist both turned back, each taking a precious high-altitude porter with them. Now it was just Derek, Dave the photographer, Seb the assistant cameraman, four porters and myself.

With dawn approaching fast, I told my cameraman and photographer to get ahead with one porter while Seb and I waited with the other three to form a climbing group for them to film when dawn broke. I had no idea how this was going to work without Rowena and Susannah, but just followed the rule of 'keep on filming and worry about it later.' Seb and I were almost frozen solid by the time dawn broke, but what an amazing sight it was. We were above the clouds and the early rays of the African sun were casting a red and orange glow on the mountain. We could see the top of Kilimanjaro just a few hundred metres away but over an hour in terms of walking zigzag at an altitude where ten steps feel like a hundred.

Derek and Dave reached the rim of the cone at around 9am to be in position to film the final hundred metres of our climb, the length of a football pitch, but then we lost them as cloud enveloped the mountain. Seb was totally consumed by altitude sickness and I wasn't far behind. We were done in, completely exhausted by our forced stoppages in freezing temperatures and then having to push the pace.

I was angry with Kilimanjaro; she had not shown her face once in three days apart from fleeting glimpses – far from the photograph that had inspired the project. We had failed, we had no ending, my head was spinning, and the only way was down, which took just twenty minutes sliding on the now unfrozen scree. Nine hours up and less than half an hour to get down. The mood remained grim all day as we trudged back to camp two, once again in mist. This time Harold had not gone ahead and reserved our accommodation, so I found a bunk with three German trekkers and fell asleep without eating.

At dawn there was a loud knocking on the door. Derek was there, camera in hand, pointing at the clear blue sky and Kilimanjaro standing proud in all her glory. 'Fuck it!' I picked up the tripod, and Derek, myself and a porter turned around and walked back up the mountain while the remaining six members of our team and

1989, KILIMANJARO, TANZANIA

CTG expedition, bottom right, nearing the
summit at dawn

their porters continued the descent. We made our way back onto the plateau and started to film all the shots of Kilimanjaro that we had not seen on our ascent, and then did so all the way down as for once the mountain was not shrouded in cloud during the day. These shots became gold dust during the edit as, every time Rowena and Susannah paused to look up, we were able to cut to a shot of the mountain that we had actually filmed on the way down. It was dark by the time Derek and I arrived at the hotel, where all the porters and Harold were gathered around a campfire waiting for their money. Despite painful blisters all round, the team had rallied and Caroline had recorded lots of singing and atmospheric effects that contributed to a vivid soundtrack.

The safari side of the adventure was an altogether different experience where we had all the weather and luck that we needed, including close-ups of a pride of lions with cubs, shimmering flocks of pink flamingos, laughing hippos, you name it. Rowena and Susannah came to life among the animals and even showed off their cosmetics to a group of young Maasai women of a similar age, until the whole village came out and turned the scene into a chaotic sea of happy faces while the impressive spear-wielding warriors looked on. We were the only passengers on the flight back to Addis and the pilot flew over Kilimanjaro for us to see if we could get an aerial shot from the window, but the mountain was covered in cloud. I arrived home two stones lighter than I went out to Africa but with sixteen hours of footage in the can.

To my surprise, Mark was keen to get on with the rest of the video catalogue before we had even started editing the African Companions film. So it was straight off to Galway Bay to film Sea Level, where seaweed farmer Peter Nolan was waiting to show Mark how to grow and harvest carrageen and other kelps that were an important natural ingredient in some of Mark's cosmetic creations. Now it was Mark's turn to experience a little of what I had endured in Africa. An Atlantic gale hit us on day one, making it both wet and dangerous to film, and it didn't relent on day two. The shoot had to be cancelled and it was time for one of those conversations that I hate having with Mark.

In my heart I knew the video catalogue was doomed; it was never a realistic idea and trying to make it work was overwhelming me. I pretty much begged Mark to drop the idea and just concentrate on making the best film we could out of the Africa footage, and mercifully he agreed. At the top of Kilimanjaro I had thought all was lost, but by filming all the trials and tribulations of the adventure, we had created a documentary drama that highlighted the lengths a company was prepared to go to in order to test its cosmetics on humans rather than on animals in a laboratory. Yes, Kilimanjaro may have defeated Rowena and Susannah, but the travel cosmetics had protected their skin in the harshest of conditions. Susannah had succumbed to hypothermia not sunburn, while Rowena had suffered altitude sickness not chapped skin.

It took a lot of editing and we pretty much used every shot, with Mark getting very involved in the process, pushing and pushing until we had the best film that we could make. The end result was released as a video that customers could buy in the autumn edition of the CTG catalogue, and we had our own premiere with red carpet and frocks at Poole Arts Centre.

Mark's strategy to grow Cosmetics To Go was essentially based around a free mail-order catalogue that came out three or four times a year. It read like a comic book, with stories and features that appealed heavily to teenage girls and their mums. The value of the products was reinforced by free post and packaging on every order, and each package was hand-wrapped and tied up with string to create the unique look of the CTG brand. It was a new way to send cosmetics as gifts, and Mark often described it as the cosmetics version of Interflora. A high volume of sales had to be achieved to offset the free catalogues, packaging and delivery costs, so building and maintaining the database of customers was crucial. This required huge amounts of publicity but not direct advertising as Mark was influenced by the same methodology employed to publicise The Body Shop.

The pivotal moment was an appearance on BBC TV's popular Sunday-night programme *The Clothes Show* hosted by Jeff Banks. He interviewed Mark and Helen around a Victorian roll-top bath in Mark's bathroom. This was no ordinary bathroom, but a large bedroom converted into a luxury bathroom with a staircase leading to an attic bedroom above it. Mark joked with Banks that they often held creative meetings around his bath, and the piece ended with a bath bomb fizzing around the bath and releasing a message that said 'Boom-Boom.' This was the original blackberry bath bomb, invented by Mo in the design of a round black cartoon bomb with a long red fuse. Almost six million viewers watched that edition of *The Clothes Show* and it had cost CTG nothing. Who needs video catalogues or PR films when you can get such excellent free TV publicity? Soon Mark, Rowena and Helen were appearing on a host of TV shows, including *The Generation Game*, a week-long stint on *The Big Breakfast*, and *Going Live*, the popular Saturday morning kids' show.

Around this time it was quite a surprise to discover that Mo was expecting another baby, after a five-year gap, and in the summer of 1990 Claire Constantine was born. Twenty-four years later she would become the first manager of the biggest and highest-grossing

1988, COSMETICS TO GO

The original Blackberry Bath Bomb – 'Boom-Boom'

Lush shop in the world, Lush Oxford Street, after serving a long apprenticeship in every corner of the business.

In December 1990, Cosmetics To Go took a large stand at the *Clothes Show Live Exhibition* at the NEC, and I was tasked with

project-managing the build of a mini shop and factory. I called in a set designer, Martin Batchell, whom I had first met when developing ideas for the video catalogue. One of Mark's truisms is that time and money spent on failed projects often turns out to be useful in the end and, while we never used

1990, NEC BIRMINGHAM
Cosmetics To Go stand at the first
Clothes Show Live Exhibition

Martin's set designs for a video, we did find a talented exhibition designer and shopfitter.

Martin created a quirky exhibition stand that looked like a cut-out brick-built structure and which we named 29½ High Street after the HQ in Poole. One end was the CTG shop, which led through to the CTG mail-order room – visited by Postman Pat himself – and then to a cutaway factory and laboratory where Mark and Helen did live presentations of product-making, something that Lush practice to this day. I suggested adding a chimney up which we could blow fragranced stage smoke that could be seen from anywhere in the NEC. It had the desired effect, and on the Saturday morning millions of *Going Live* viewers watched Mark being interviewed while making a product

1990, NEC BIRMINGHAM
Postman Pat on the CTG stand

live on the stand.

The following summer Mark participated in a summer edition of *The Clothes Show* highlighting the effectiveness of seaweed in healing sunburn. The BBC set up a Victorian bath on a Newquay beach, and sunburnt tourists laid in the bath as Mark cooled their skin with kelp while being interviewed by Brenda Emmanus.

1991, NEWQUAY, CORNWALL
Mark on the beach filming for The Clothes Show

*The Clothes Show Live Exhibition* became a regular feature of the CTG publicity machine, and it got bigger and bigger each year. But why take a miniature shop and factory to the NEC only in December when you can open your own factory to the public as a tourist attraction? I'm sure it was frequent visits to Disneyland that gave Mark the idea to open his factory to the public during the summer tourist season. His young manufacturing staff took to the idea with great enthusiasm, as is often the case with Mark's big ideas, and they made it work. My contribution was to produce a short film featuring all the parts of the business the public could not see – the specialist outworkers, the mail-order office, the fulfilment unit with Parcel Force collecting the parcels – and to screen it in a bespoke mini-cinema in the factory adjacent to the final showstopper attraction.

During all this time Mo had been modestly inventing new ways of making soap. Now she set herself a target to get into the *Guinness Book of Records* by making the world's largest soap. It was made in the design of an open CTG parcel with a selection of CTG soaps bursting out of the top. Everything was made of soap, right down to the string and labels, as Mo had worked out ways to pour

1992, COSMETICS TO GO EXPERIENCE
Mo with the worlds largest soap in its mould

both hot and cold soaps into shapes. It was huge – over two metres high and weighing over four tons – and it had to be moulded 'in position' in the final room of the factory tour. I filmed the soap sculpture when it was completed, and added the sequence to the 1950s style *Look at Life* newsreel that I had created for the cinema.

Visitors reached the soap via an electronic garage door between the cinema and the soap, which opened at the end of the film with a show of disco lights and coloured smoke, before they filed out of the cinema and into the exhibit. This was after they had entered the factory through a hanging garden and been treated to the Cosmetic To Go Experience including tours of the various rooms and manufacturing techniques.

Mo's soap did get into the *Guinness Book of Records* and was finally cut up by a *Home and Away* 'soap'opera star, Richard Norton, with a chainsaw. Mo has always enjoyed a good play on words and has penned many of the names of CTG and Lush products.

By 1993 Mark was at the height of his creative energies. The ideas just got bigger and bolder. For the second season of the factory tour he demanded a film in 'smellyvision', but omitted to inform me that the cinema was now a manufacturing room and I'd have to rebuild it in the middle of the factory. Working with Jeff Brown, Mark's long-standing perfumer, we initially thought of a film that

illustrated the three main notes of a perfume: top or head notes, middle or heart notes, and base notes. I had visions of a concert pianist playing notes on a piano while we wafted the cinema with these scents, but it soon became clear that once we introduced multiple fragrances the olfactory nerves of the audience would become saturated and unable to distinguish one scent from another. This is why smellyvision had not worked in Hollywood, where cinemas in the 1950s had experimented with introducing the aroma of fast food, like hot dogs, but had found the smell just lingered and was absorbed by the soft furnishings.

Jeff reckoned we should limit ourselves to just a single heart note, the classic fragrance of rose, which would evaporate fairly quickly, and so he set about getting permission for us to film at a supplier in Morocco. Meanwhile, I commissioned a local company to build a system to spray the fragrance into the factory cinema and an extraction system to clear the air in time for the next audience. It also needed to have plastic seats and no soft furnishings. Oh, and it all had to work at the press of a button.

In the spring of 1993 I headed off to Morocco with Jeff and my film crew, still harbouring some anxieties after my previous trip to Africa. I need not have worried, the Moroccan Film Board helped me all the way: proper permits, no bribes and a dedicated minibus driver who looked after us from the moment we landed to the moment we left.

The fields on the slopes of the Atlas Mountains were bursting with *rosa centifolia*, from which rose absolute is made. As directed by our French hosts, we were standing among the roses at 6am, after leaving our hotel in Rabat in the hours of darkness. It was beautiful and perfectly calm, with the dew still fresh on the petals, which was very important. A gong sounded and suddenly the whole village swarmed into the plantation, the women and girls working their way down the rows of cultivated roses, while the men and boys brought carts along the lanes. Everywhere there was a shot to be had of smiling women picking rose petals and filling the slings draped around their shoulders. The younger girls made garlands for their hair and every so often they emptied their slings into large sacks on the carts. It went on for several hours before the sun got too high and dried the petals. The women picked tons of rose petals in those few hours and then back in the village we saw how they were paid for their work, as well as the process by which the oil was extracted from the petals to form a liquid that set solid as rose concrete, the building block of rose absolute, which featured in many CTG products.

'Smellyvision' was a total success. Visitors to the CTG factory tour entered the cinema and, at the push of a button, saw the big screen burst into life with beautiful sequences of the rose harvest intertwined with a story told by a woman taking a candlelit bath (in Mark's Victorian bath). The microprocessor in the control unit fired off the spray guns at the correct moment so the audience could

smell the roses they were seeing, and we gave them a piece of Turkish delight to eat during the show as it also contains rose oil. It was a complete sensual experience that had seemed impossible when Mark initially suggested it, and in the end it was worthy of an award!

1993, ATLAS MOUNTAINS, MOROCCO
Rose harvesting for 'Smellyvision'

Throughout this period, Britain had been sliding into recession, and by 1990 unemployment had got back to three million. You would never have known you were in a recession at CTG, however, as the sales orders just kept piling up, in stark contrast to what was being experienced by many other industries. My own media industry was in serious decline and many of the large corporate video producers were going bust.

By the summer of 1993 the recession was at its peak, but Cosmetics To Go was still growing fast, or so it appeared. Frequent postal strikes were an ongoing problem but CTG was also having issues with customer fulfilment, so Mark asked me to make a training film to get the 'customers first' message across to staff. Using letters of complaint, I tracked down customers around the country who were prepared to articulate their views on the levels of service they were experiencing, both good and bad. I also conceived a hard-hitting opening scene depicting the company going bust, with a deserted run-down factory, and a 'For Sale' notice being hammered into the ground. It was designed to get the attention of the staff, but it turned out to be the harbinger of things to come.

The runaway train of Cosmetics To Go was now at full speed, yet people were still getting on board. Whole families had built small businesses out of working for CTG, suppliers were queueing to get in on the action, and Mark had hired a marketing consultant who was upping the ante even higher. My former boss Clive Holmes was now the designer of the iconic Cosmetics To Go catalogues, and he was given instructions to increase the frequency and circulation of these free-to-the-customer publications. I was called into a meeting with Pearl & Dean to discuss the production of a cinema advert for Cosmetics To Go, despite the fact that Mark does not do direct advertising – not then, not now, not ever.

Something was amiss, but Mark was powering on and ordered the biggest ever stand at the Clothes Show Live Exhibition, which had now moved to Earl's Court. The summer sale was a huge success, but so big was the demand that it overwhelmed the computer system, and indeed every system. Hilary Jones – today Lush's Ethics Director – had just joined the company as a mailroom worker and remembers piles of cheques and order forms building up, as well as vouchers promising customers a free product for every new customer they introduced, whether they were real or made

1993, COSMETICS TO GO PARCEL ROOM

Ashley under pressure with orders waiting for delivery

up. Some customers received the same parcel twice. My 'customers first' training video was shelved for fear of demoralising an already overworked staff. Cosmetics To Go was running out of cash as the true cost of free post and packaging hit home.

Mark was already looking for a white knight to inject much-needed cash into the business. In fact, Mark and Karl had met with the high-street fashion retailer Next and shaken on a deal, with the managing director, David Jones. Unknown to both of them, Next was in discussions with the American retail chain Bath & Body Works, and so it's not hard to see why Cosmetics To Go would be a useful acquisition – possibly one that could be stripped of all its valuable assets such as the products and patents.

The final third of the £9 million payment from The Body Shop was not due until 1994, but the company had run up a £2 million overdraft at Lloyds Bank, which Mark was forced to pay off by an unsympathetic bank calling in its large debts in the face of a recession. This left Cosmetics To Go with no working capital but in his defence, Mark took advice from his accountants, who advised him that with £3 million still owed, CTG was not insolvent and that he could still trade.

In December, the scale of the Cosmetics To Go stand at the Clothes Show Live exhibition at Earls Court was bigger than ever and spanned two stands with a connecting arch. But there was a different mood to the place; the fun had gone out of the show and CTG customers weren't spending. If Mark was hoping a successful Clothes Show, or Next, would save him, he was sadly mistaken.

On Christmas Day, with no one around, a radiator pipe burst in the locked

1993, COSMETICS TO GO
The final CTG mail-order catalogue

offices of Joliffe House, the administrative headquarters of Cosmetics To Go in Poole. Late in the evening the police called Mark to inform him the alarm was sounding. Water had been flowing through the building, possibly for up to twenty-four hours. Ceilings had collapsed and every room of the three-floor building had been destroyed. The phone room, the computers, and all the paperwork and records of the mail-order company were lost in the flood. Mark and Mo were staring ruin in the face.

Next did not come through with an offer to buy the business, and on 17th January 1994, on the advice of his accountants, Mark called in the receivers. A lot of small suppliers, such as Martin who designed and built the Clothes Show exhibition stand, were going to be wiped out. Clive was also into CTG for a serious amount of money, having produced the Christmas catalogue, but I thought he would have bad debt insurance. Martin did not, and he told me that he wouldn't piss on Mark if he was on fire in the street. I told Mark what he had said, and years later, when Lush became successful, he made a point of giving Martin plenty of shopfitting work by way of atonement.

The months following the receivership were just one long funeral procession. Mark did not talk about the collapse much, in fact I barely saw him. I presumed he had enough money to tide him over; after all, he now owned two houses, a shop and a factory unit, but all with substantial mortgages. He was forced to sell his £200,000 weekend house by the sea in Swanage at a £100,000 loss, and, to make matters worse, the elevated rear garden of the property had collapsed onto the beach huts below, requiring a £45,000 repair job. He could not find a buyer for either 29 High Street or the factory unit – a blessing in disguise as it turned out. However, all of his staff were now unemployed, including his partners. Despite the business raking in £6 million from The Body Shop, the suppliers made more out of Cosmetics To Go than Mark or any of his partners because they just paid themselves a normal annual salary. The final £3 million went in £2 million worth of fees for the official receiver, leaving just £1 million to be shared out among the creditors at a penny for every pound. I'm surprised Mark ever trusted a bank and a firm of accountants ever again.

So what do you do when the company you have built up over seventeen years goes bust, your partners and all of your employees have been made redundant, and you have mortgages to pay on redundant buildings but without any income? You do what Mark has always done to get away from the worry and stress of running a business: you go birding!

# <sup>11</sup> Twitch

It's impossible to write a biography of Mark Constantine without talking about his passion for birding. It is as much a part of his life as his business ventures; indeed, he has now turned it into a niche business in its own right, known as The Sound Approach. Once he caught the bug for birding there was no looking back. Within a very short time of his seminal Brecon Beacons holiday in 1974, he had resurrected the Dorset Bird Club, and was making friends with Bill Oddie, the well-known 'Goodie', ornithologist and long-time presenter of the BBC wildlife programme *Nature Watch*. Today Mark is on equally good terms with Chris Packham, the current presenter of *Springwatch* and *Autumnwatch*, and Mark has enthusiastically supported some of his independent campaigning work.

Mark has always had the ability to compartmentalise his life, so in the early days he would generally spend a third of his time manufacturing from home, a third treating clients at the Herbal Hair and Beauty Clinic, and a third birding which, from spring through autumn, would be most weekends, every holiday and a lot of early mornings.

In 1980 Mark was birding off Portland with his friend John Leadwood when they saw at some distance a large seabird with black edges to its wings, which they could not identify. Mark phoned a fellow birder, who told him that the new warden of Durlston

Country Park near Swanage, Hamish Murray, had recently seen a black-browed albatross off the cliffs at Durlston Head. This was a very rare sighting for the Dorset coast as, like all albatrosses, the black-browed albatross is primarily a bird of the southern oceans. Keen to establish if the bird he saw twenty miles further down the coast might also have been the albatross, Mark phoned Hamish and thus began a long friendship.

Hamish was and still is a knowledgeable all-round naturalist, bird artist and an occasional musician. As warden of the country park, he and his wife Barb lived on the job in the warden's bungalow, an idyllic location in summer but rather remote on a wild winter's night. A quietly spoken Scot, Hamish opened up the world of birding for Mark, particularly when it came to identifying birds by their calls or song, and in those early years you could pretty much guarantee that if Mark was not at home or at work, he was in Swanage, birding with Hamish. Indeed, Mark would often get up early in the morning and cycle fifteen miles in the dark to get to Durlston Country Park before the dawn chorus, and then cycle back to Poole a few hours later to work in his home factory or at the clinic.

Another friend and mentor who helped to nurture Mark's passion for birding was Peter Grant, a hugely influential figure in British birding at the time, and as affable and sociable as he was knowledgeable, especially when it came to the more challenging aspects of bird identification. Mark first met him in 1984 in Mallorca, where Peter led bird tours during the spring migration season. He was chairman of the British Birds Rarities Committee and an editor of the long-established journal *British Birds.* As Mark acknowledges in his 2006 book *The Sound Approach to birding*, 'I was very keen to learn and he was a great teacher. After his tour-leading duties, he would sit with Mo and me, drinking wine and teach us about moult, topography, and identification.'

Mark continued to take annual holidays in Mallorca, where Peter introduced him to Killian Mullarney, the renowned Irish bird artist and co-author of the highly acclaimed *Collins Bird Guide.* Killian's illustrations can be found in many authoritative identification papers, several books and on numerous postage stamps issued by the Irish Post Office; in short, he is regarded as one of the foremost experts on bird identification in Europe. In the late 1980s, he and Peter co-authored a series of papers entitled *The New Approach to Identification,* first published in *Birding World* magazine, and regarded as a highly informative introduction to the more fundamental aspects of field-observation and identification of birds. It was no coincidence that when Mark published his first book, *The Sound Approach to birding*, it had a similar title, was dedicated to the late Peter Grant and illustrated by Killian Mullarney.

2018, BIRDS OF POOLE HARBOUR, POOLE QUAY

A selection of *The Sound Approach* series of books and accompanying CDs

There was a lot of birding to do over the preceding fifteen
years to enable Mark to take his interest in bird calls and sounds
to the point where he could write and publish books about the
subject. However, from the moment Mark met Hamish, then Peter
and Killian, his interest in learning and transcribing bird sounds
became obsessive, and as a successful businessman he had the deep
pockets to fund his birding adventures.

In 1990 he teamed up with Killian and three other international birders to take part in the World Series of Birding race, which
was held in New Jersey, USA. Calling themselves the Transatlantic Vagrants, they competed against around eighty other teams of
dedicated birders to see who could identify the most birds in the

1990, NEW JERSEY, USA

The Transatlantic Vagrants — (Left to Right) Bruce Mactavish, Mark, Anthony McGeehan, Ian Hodgson
& Killian Mullarmey

state of New Jersey in a twenty-four-hour period. Mark had to familiarise himself with the sounds of over a hundred unfamiliar North American bird species to be able to contribute usefully to the team effort, but he is very good at focusing on something to the exclusion of all else.

1994, WOODLAND, NEW JERSEY
Mark birding with the SASS mounted on his tripod

The Transatlantic Vagrants were sponsored by and raced around in a brand-new Jaguar. They also got shot at while tramping around the New Jersey countryside, no doubt for having strayed into a farmer's field without permission. Within two years Mark was captain of the team and he invited Arnoud B van den Berg, the editor of *Dutch Birding* to join them. Arnoud was a well-known bird photographer but, unknown to Mark at the time, he was also a highly experienced bird-sound recordist, with over 4,000 recordings for Cornell University to his name. Over the next seven springs of the World Series of Birding fortnight, Mark shared a room with Arnoud and learned a great deal about recording bird sounds, as well as the Dutch sense of humour.

One day I visited Mark at home to find him playing with a large black-winged box and a pair of Sennheiser microphones. He told me that it was called an SASS (Stereo Ambient Sampling System), which he could mount on his tripod next to his telescope and record the birds he was watching. Having recently completed my first ever film in Dolby surround sound, I was intrigued by this piece of kit as stereo sound recording is technically challenging and requires a high level of skill. Although Mark could easily afford the best equipment, I wasn't sure that he could become a competent sound recordist. Nevertheless, he lugged this kit around the world as he learned the hard way how to record bird sound.

Let me just add here that he was not after a simple 'tu-whit tu-whoo' to identify a tawny owl, he was interested in recording the full repertoire of all birds, throughout the seasons, with particular attention to establishing the correct species identification and, where possible, the age and sex of the subject. The goal was to build up a comprehensive catalogue of bird sounds that would enable birders to identify birds by call or song, and also learn how to 'read' or interpret visual representations of the sounds in the form of sonograms, graphs that show the various frequencies and timings of the recorded sound.

Mark had learned the art of reading sonograms from one of his World Series of Birding teammates, Bruce Mactavish, while birding together in America. To put it in layman's terms if you see a bird close up you can generally identify it by its outward features, as well as its call or song; if it's in the distance and particularly if it's a small bird hidden in the hedgerow, the call or song is often the only means of precise identification. However, there are often subtle variations in the sounds of very similar birds, such as the

2005, KENNEMERMEER, IJMUIDEN, NETHERLANDS

Recording bird sounds with the Telinga parabolic microphone

many types of warblers, so if you have learned the visual shape of the sonogram – the highs and lows, the inflection and tone – you might be able to say 'That's a Siberian chiff-chaff' without actually seeing it. That is a hugely over simplified way of describing what Mark and his Sound Approach team were trying to achieve. As it turned out, the expensive stereo recording system that Mark had purchased at great cost was still not good enough to record the subtleties of bird sounds when faced with all the other ambient sounds like aircraft noise, tractors in the fields, wind noise and even other birders farting too close to the mic!

Arnoud and the newest team member, Magnus Robb, were using the Swedish-made Telinga wildlife microphone with its trademark transparent parabolic dish – spy microphones to you and me, the use of which in a sensitive location is a reason to be arrested in some parts of the world. Today Mark and his Sound Approach team have recorded and curated one of the most comprehensive collections of bird recordings in the world. They are even credited with discovering a new species of owl, in Oman.

All of Mark's birding kit lies strewn around his home, together with an extensive birding library and a collection of bird art that leaves you in no doubt as to where his main interest lies. When his house was broken into some years ago only a laptop, camera and memory sticks were stolen, despite thousands of pounds worth of binoculars, telescopes and recording equipment on open view. One can only conclude that the thief had no interest in monetary value but only in the information on Mark's laptop that might prove useful to another cosmetics company or, dare I say it, the dark side of the law.

Perhaps the character trait in Mark that explains his success is his ability to focus on a few things and become expert at them. If you spend 10,000 hours practising the violin, you'll become an accomplished violinist, and Mark has spent a lot more than 10,000 hours watching and recording birds. Unlike me, he does not get physically involved with DIY, gardening, motor mechanics or sport, unless you include table football, which bizarrely he is very good at.

As a filmmaker what I love about birding is the people who make this all- consuming hobby so characterful. Mark has dragged

Birders meeting in the Blue Boar pub

me to the British Bird Fair, Bird Club meetings, birding boat trips around Poole Harbour, and any number of dinner parties at his house full of birders. They can talk for hours on the minutest detail of an individual bird, or the highs and lows of an important 'twitch' (seeing a rare bird for the first time) with the intensity of a G20 summit. While for many, the pursuit of the rarity may be what they put most of their energy into, most birders are also passionate advocates of conservation and species-protection. The precipitous decline of the Montagu's harrier as a British breeding bird – a direct consequence of illegal and relentless persecution by gamekeepers working on grouse moors – is tantamount to a declaration of war to birders. Mark encouraged a Lush conservation campaign to lobby the Queen after a satellite-tagged Montagu's harrier named 'Mo' disappeared on a royal estate in Norfolk.

Protection of the Montagu's harrier has also been a passion of Chris Packham along with his well documented campaign to stop the shooting of migrating birds on Malta and Cyprus, where trigger-happy islanders shoot first and identify afterwards. It is unmitigated slaughter and has no place in any modern European country. Chris has been a speaker at Lush conferences and he is utterly engaging, even more so when you are aware that he suffers from Asperger's Syndrome, a disorder characterised by significant difficulties in social interaction and non-verbal communication. That is an equally good way of describing birders; given a choice between going to a party or going birding, or even just talking about birding, birding wins every time. Apparently they call it Asbirder's Syndrome.

In 2016 Mark and his birding colleagues embarked on the creation of Birds of Poole Harbour, which they describe as 'a charity completely dedicated to educating people on the stunning variety of bird life in one of the country's most picturesque locations.' In the summer of 2017, Birds of Poole Harbour began a five-year osprey translocation project with the aim of re-establishing this once-common bird to its former breeding grounds. Eight osprey chicks were relocated to purpose-built nesting sites in Arne, where they grew into young adults. The ospreys were electronically tagged, and since migrating in the autumn of 2017 two have been located in Africa. Hopefully they and some of the others will return to Poole Harbour and start breeding.

2018, POOLE QUAY
Birds of Poole Harbour Information Centre

The charity is funded by Mark and Mo until such time as it is self-sustaining. Mark is heavily involved with all aspects of the charity, which includes leading popular bird boat tours for local schools. Birds of Poole Harbour now has its own bespoke information centre on Poole Quay, where visitors can see live webcams of various sites around the harbour and talk to enthusiastic volunteers. Indeed Mark can now stand on Poole Quay and see both the Lush global headquarters and the Birds of Poole Harbour information centre without having to turn his head.

# THE COSMETEERS RETURN

Helen Ambrosen, Mark Constantine, Liz Wier, Paul Greeves, Mo Constantine, Mike Bird, Ro Hofbau

We have a policy of buying only from companies that use alternatives to animal tests for the safety of raw materials.
*This is easy when the main supplier is Jan & John the fruit and veg wholesalers.*

All the products are vegetarian

we love our work, and this shows in the product
cant believe we said that !

effective **and** safe **to use.** We do not **use** mineral oil **and this makes a** considerable difference to our creams, lotions and bath oils.

Everything is made and wrapped by hand.

You can visit the shop at 29½ High Street, Poole or, order by post and send us a cheque

Tested on humans

dates of manufacture of the liquid products are on the label as are the ingredients.
(not 50ml)

We are delighted to sell our cosmetics wholesale. So if you want to start a shop, have parties, start a cool (probably cold) market stall, call us.

# <u>12</u> The Cosmeteers Return

I felt bad about attending the final act of Cosmetics To Go, the winding-up sale of all the assets at the factory. I was hoping to buy back the cinema equipment for future use but it had mysteriously disappeared. We still didn't see any sign of Mark or Mo getting jobs but I was pretty sure neither of them signed on at the local jobcentre. It wasn't the sort of question we liked to ask, as we already knew they were being forced to sell their Swanage house at a big loss while trying to placate a bunch of agitated beach-hut owners. Additionally, the rights to the Cosmetics To Go name had been picked up by one of Mark's former suppliers and they were trying to run a much smaller version of the mail-order business from a small unit on the outskirts of Poole. The death of a company that you have built up over seventeen years is hard to deal with, particularly when people who made nice money out of you during the good times now blame you for their decision to put all their eggs in one basket.

Mark told me that the day he signed the winding-up papers for Cosmetics To Go was the worst day of his life; the official administrator didn't even shake his hand when offered. Years later, Mark learned that he didn't need to put the company in the hands of official receivers. Cosmetics To Go was not insolvent, it had just run out of working capital and he could have used the final £3 million payment from The Body Shop to pay off all his creditors in full and close down the company himself.

None of the founders of Cosmetics To Go had found meaningful work since the official winding-up order in April 1994, although at one stage Rowena's passion for hot-air ballooning was tempting her to join Per Lindstrand's company Lindstrand Balloons. It was Helen who started the ball rolling again, suggesting to a reluctant Mark that they had some ingredients, pots and pans knocking around the place, and they still had a shop. (The Body Shop's embargo on Mark opening a cosmetic retail shop had expired by this point.) Paul Greeves, the Cosmetics To Go IT manager, had found a job in the NHS, but left after a week, and demanded his old job back, even though it meant working for free. He still had a back-up copy of their previous mail-order database and was keen to reactivate it. Together this was a recipe for some sort of small retail shop and mail-order business, so Mark and the rest of the founders, now including Paul, put their aprons back on and started making cosmetics again.

Rowena weighed in with her credit card and soon-to-be-husband, Mike Bird, and together they fitted out the old CTG shop at 29 High Street, albeit in the most basic way. All the signs were handwritten on blackboards, the packaging of the new products was minimal – all forced on the fledgling business by a lack of funds, a bit like the start of The Body Shop. The big difference was that the quality of the products on offer remained as high as ever, so when Cosmetic House opened in the winter of 1994, the most loyal of Cosmetics To Go's former customers returned to their beloved supplier. I took a press photograph of the founders on the opening day in black and white. It was such a stark contrast to the colourful world of Cosmetics To Go, and it felt like they had all got into a time machine in 1988 and returned back from the future.

This was the start of Lush: one shop, six founders and a mailing list of about 2,000 customers. The catalogue was just newsprint on recycled paper; they couldn't afford to include many photographs. Also, they ran a competition among the customers to come up with a trading name and the winner was a Mrs Bennett with 'Lush Garden', which they shortened to Lush. A cartoon-style green and yellow logo was designed by Jo Evans, which did hark back to CTG, but it was the only flash of colour in the brand. Jo, an art student who had just finished her studies, was the first paid employee of the new company. She evolved the style of Lush, including the handwritten blackboards, and continues to do so, to this day.

With its one shop, it was a hand-to-mouth existence, but Mark was in discussions with a venture capitalist, Peter Blacker, who apparently owned an estate complete with a castle in Scotland. A former customer of Cosmetics To Go, Andrew Gerrie had been a great fan of the company and had identified Mark as a person worth investing in. Andrew, who worked for Peter, was the conduit between Mark and the money man, and eventu-

1994, POOLE

Lush logo designed by Jo Evans

ally became a director and significant shareholder in Lush.

Mark and Andrew's plan centred on opening retail shops inside the M25, figuring that if the business didn't take off in Greater London it wouldn't work anywhere. Footfall was the key and they started with a small unit in the old Covent Garden flower market, now a major tourist attraction and retail outlet in its own right. That must have appealed immensely to Mark, as he is a huge fan of Audrey Hepburn, famous for her role as the cockney flower-seller Eliza Doolittle in the film version of *My Fair Lady*. I can imagine Mark singing 'Wouldn't it be Loverly?' in the bath as he contemplated his first proper shop in Covent Garden.

The market-trader style of Lush had already been established in Poole, but now Mark and Andrew had the opportunity to try it out in the most famous market in London. Unpackaged bath bombs were displayed like apples and oranges, giant-sized soaps were stacked like selections of cheeses. Lush Covent Garden was the cosmetic equivalent of a grocer's store – something that would have undoubtedly met with the approval of Mark's maternal grandfather, a grocer himself.

Thanks to The Body Shop, natural cosmetics wasn't something new, but Lush offered a new way of buying them. Lush was everything that mainstream cosmetics was not: raw, unpackaged, hands-on, fresh from the factory. You could smell the shop before you reached it, just like a bakery. Indeed, some customers actually thought you could eat some of the products.

As you entered the shop you picked up a wicker basket while the Lush equivalent of Eliza Doolittle in her or his apron told you all about the 'loverly' products on display, the inspiration behind the products, and their ingredients while giving you samples to try and

1995, LUSH SHOP DISPLAY
Soaps stacked like cheeses

weighing out your slices of soap. All the lessons learned from the failure of Cosmetics To Go were now focused on providing the best customer-service experience on the high street, so that soon everyone was talking about that little cosmetics shop in Covent Garden.

The following year it became two shops in London, with the opening of a larger store on the Kings Road in Chelsea, another iconic shopping area with a high footfall and an upmarket clientele, including royalty. Rowena managed the shop in its early days and lived in the flat over the store. To have a founder managing the Lush Kings Road shop ensured plenty of publicity for the fledgling business as Rowena was well qualified to speak to journalists and appear on daytime television to demonstrate products. She was also receiving a thousand enquiries a month from people wanting to open a Lush shop!

Gradually, as confidence increased, Mark began bringing many former employees back in to run the manufacturing operations in Poole, and also attracting new retail sales people like Lizzie Edgar, the first manager of Lush Covent Garden, who still works for the company and has trained hundreds of managers over the years. Gordon Roddick told Mark that when The Body Shop went public, he and Anita lost control of the business and the people running it. He had admired Mark's ability to build a strong team at Constantine & Weir, and now many of them were waiting to rejoin the new business.

Unlike Cosmetics To Go, money was not frittered away at Lush; in fact, nothing was wasted if it could possibly be recycled or reused in some way. Behind the scenes there was a much more structured business plan and financial discipline. Mark had learned his lesson from the collapse of CTG and was determined not to repeat the same mistakes with Lush.

Over the next couple of years, Lush moved to a larger shop in Covent Garden and opened stores outside of London in tourist towns like Chester, the new Lakeside retail park and on Princes Street in Glasgow. In the capital they opened another shop on Carnaby Street, again an area where a high volume of passing customers was guaranteed and where the 'flower-sellers' at the door of the now bright yellow and green stores would entice them in to sample their wares.

Around this time a former Body Shop manager Simon Nicholls, who had worked for Deb McCormick in Bath, approached Mark and offered to work for free. Mark had to ask him to go away for a few hours while he thought up a job for him. UK Retail Sales

Manager became his title but he probably did not earn the salary that might be expected to go with it. Simon is now a director at Lush where he has developed much of the overseas business and, as an avid guitarist, he became the resident songwriter for Lush TV ten years later.

As Mark started on his way back up, I too experienced a stroke of good fortune. By the end of 1995 pretty much all of my media customers had gone to the wall in one form or another. However, the previous year I had written a speculative treatment for a potential client in London and then heard nothing. Suddenly the project was back on again and a few months later I was in South Africa filming the first of many health and safety films for a global company servicing the iron and steel industry. It was a relationship that would last for the next 15 years and take me all over the world.

Meanwhile, Mark was beginning the international roll-out of Lush. The shops in Covent Garden and the Kings Road had proved to be an inspiration to visitors from overseas, people who could see the potential in their own countries.

The first approach came from Slavica Caleta, a businesswoman in Croatia who did a deal with Mark and Andrew and then regularly sent a van to the UK to load up with Lush products. Mark described it as like something out of the TV sitcom *Only Fools and Horses*, but it was a very successful enterprise and Lush Croatia went on to become a beacon for the expansion of Lush into the EU and beyond. Today, Lush has a manufacturing facility in Croatia to service the region and another in Germany, which propitiously opened just before Britain voted to leave the EU.

Hot on the heels of Lush Croatia was a Canadian couple, Karen and Mark Wolverton, who is now the CEO of Lush North America. Mark was already a successful businessman in his own right, but not in the world of retail. It was his wife Karen who fell in love with Lush and saw the potential for a little business of her own. The first shop opened in Denman Street, Vancouver in April 1996, serviced by a small factory set up by manufacturing staff sent over to Canada from the UK. The first US store opened in San Francisco in 2002, and today Lush North America has more than 250 stores across Canada and the USA, with manufacturing facilities in Vancouver and Toronto.

Most of this information Mark would tell me over tea and biscuits in his kitchen dining room – his real kitchen, the one he built to replace the one he turned into a home factory in 1982. Many significant events have taken place in this space, dominated by a large dining table around which you can seat the cabinet of a small country. On any given day, on the table there will be a large bowl of fruit, a vase of flowers, various items of birding paraphernalia, a Time Manager containing Mark's notes, the latest Apple laptop and iPhone, and piles of cards and letters. More business has been transacted over this table, while simultaneously keeping an eye on the bird feeders in the garden, than I care to recount. There is a constant flow of people in and out of the kitchen, from members of his extended family to builders, gardeners and birders, sometimes all at the same time. If you think that the head of a billion-pound international company works from a plush office in a glass tower, think again. Mark is invariably at home in the kitchen or in his lab at 29 High Street – if he is not out birding or travelling on Lush business. And if he is, it will be second-class on a train or economy in the air. He once saw a partner of his former accountancy firm, the ones that wound up CTG, get into a first-class coach at the station and Mark told him that's why they had lost his business. That's not to say that Mark did not have a top accountancy firm working for Lush. Indeed, keeping control of the finances was the biggest lesson of all from the failure of Cosmetics To Go.

By the late 1990s the organic growth of Lush was about to ride the crest of the New Labour wave, which saw ten years of uninterrupted growth in the UK. With shops opening faster and faster, training was becoming time-consuming. Mark and Liz Bennett (née Weir) did a lot of this themselves, doing whole training days at individual shops and without much in the way of bespoke visual aids. By summer 1998 it was time to splash a bit of cash my way.

Undoubtedly the most successful and utilised of all my films for Mark had been the rose harvest in Morocco. This buying trip showed staff where the raw materials came from and how they were processed into the fragrance contained in the products they were selling. 'Let's make some more!' said Mark one day around the kitchen table. We decided on lavender, and Karl was tasked with speaking to their French supplier with a view to filming the lavender harvest in Provence in July.

We were lucky enough to capture both the modern method and the traditional way of harvesting lavender and distilling it in small distilleries set amongst an unending carpet of purple flowers on the rolling hills of Haute Provence. To this I added an animation of what was happening inside the distillation vessel as the steam carried the waterborne fragrance into the Florentine flask where it cooled, and the essential oil rose to the top. It was a very atmospheric film about a high-quality Lush ingredient found in one of their bestselling soaps.

The following year we travelled to Florida to film the making of orange essential oil, which is pressed out of the skin and pith of sweet oranges grown mainly for making orange juice. It was thirsty work, but the end result was another highly visual documentary to show to Lush staff in their training sessions.

We now had three very good buying trips in the can; could these be expanded into a something bigger? Mark proposed that we make three training films based around a bestselling product that contained the essential oils we had captured on film. No.1 was *Tisty Tosty*, the popular rose-fragranced, heart-shaped bomb; No.2 was

*Sea Veg* the bestselling soap that contained seaweed and lavender oil; and No.3 was *Fresh*, the new range of veggie face masks that Helen had developed and which were made fresh in the shops each day and given a use-by date.

For many years I had been a huge fan of *Eurotrash*, a thirty-minute magazine programme presented by Antoine de Caunes and Jean-Paul Gaultier. I loved the deliberately quirky, low-budget style, the use of green-screen graphic backgrounds and the offbeat features of European life. I thought this type of approach would suit Lush, where fun was a byword for the way staff interacted with their customers. Also, by using a green-screen set, I could keep costs down and film all three editions in one day. All I needed was an inspiring presenter with a big smile.

With all her experience of appearing on broadcast TV shows like *The Big Breakfast* for CTG, Rowena was now highly accomplished at presenting to camera, and she needed no persuading. We shot all the films back-to-back, and inserted features into our magazine-style shows, including our buying trips, product-making demonstrations, and product-selling techniques to use when demonstrating the products in store. We even added a European flavour by getting the new Lush partner in Italy, Marco, to voice the three buying trips in his Italian-accented English. We produced three highly watchable magazine-style training programmes, which felt like the start of Lush TV, like Body Shop TV. Once a fortnight? Once a month? OK how about every quarter? The videos were used over and over for training Lush staff.

As we approached the end of the century, there was no doubting that Lush was on the high street to stay. The computers did not stop working at midnight on New Year's Eve, and by June 2000 Lush had grown to forty-five shops in six countries, with a turnover of £21 million. Eventually, in 2003 Mark decided it was time to update the training videos. 'I should hope so, after a four year gap', but only to give them a new look and add a few extra editions. It's hard to reinvent a format that has already worked well and, not surprisingly, Mark did not like the new look. In fact, he hated it to the point where he gave me the biggest bawling-out of my career. I hadn't seen him get so angry or use so many expletives since the day I refused to share a bedsit with him in Kensington. He found something to criticise in all of the rough cuts Rowena and I showed him, and it was some time before I got to the truth of the matter. One was that we should never have changed the format; the other, well, that's a bit more delicate.

Mark and Mo have never been great at preparing for their TV appearances, and it is usually a case of 'you take us as you find us.' He won't thank me for saying this but by 2003 the dynamic Mark Constantine of Cosmetics To Go fame, had become very overweight and was looking older than his fifty-three years. The time and energy that he and his co-founders had put into resurrecting Lush from the ashes of CTG, followed by eight years of growing it into a successful international company, had caught up with them. They were burnt out and when Mark saw himself and the others in the new training videos, it confirmed what he already knew.

He put a moratorium on any of the founders appearing on camera, and promptly closed the door on any further video production at Lush for another three years. However, the incident forced Mark to change to a healthier lifestyle; he gave up drinking more than a glass of wine at parties and events, and over the next eighteen months he lost thirty-two kilos in weight. He didn't want to become a person he despised when he looked in the mirror, or worse, someone who lost the respect of his staff.

Mark has always been a very driven entrepreneur but he is also slightly paranoid about having a heart attack after believing that both his maternal grandparents died from one. On the other hand, he has always had a fondness for biscuits and peanuts and, as a colleague once told him, being slim doesn't necessarily make you happy – it just lowers the risk of a coronary event.

Compared to Mark I was very fit, having been an amateur football referee for many years. That all changed, when I had a sudden and 'silent' heart attack during a youth league game, which left me gasping for air but thankfully still on my feet. An angiogram confirmed that I had severe coronary heart disease, which required a quadruple heart bypass. When I told Mark this, he was deeply shocked – and not for the first time that year.

A few months earlier, in March 2006, Gordon and Anita Roddick sold The Body Shop to the French cosmetics giant L'Oreal for £652 million, making them a personal fortune of around £130 million. Mark was beyond angry, he was outraged. L'Oreal was part-owned by Nestlé, which had a reputation for animal testing and a record of countless ethical shortfalls, including 130 World Health Organisation violations. How could Anita – Mark's inspiration and champion of the cruelty-free and ethical trading policies that he had helped to shape – let down the staff and customers of The Body Shop in this way? Mark felt betrayed and was openly critical of the Roddicks, especially as he had tried to buy The Body Shop when he knew it was up for sale, although Lush's offer fell some way short of £652 million. He wasn't aware at the time that Anita had contracted Hepatitis C from a blood transfusion during the birth of her daughter Sam in 1971, and her future was uncertain.

Mark told me that the loss of The Body Shop to L'Oreal felt like having his heart ripped out, something that was about to happen to me quite literally in a few months' time. Once my diagnosis had been confirmed, he tried to convince me to visit one of his homeopathic doctors in Harley Street. Mark does not like hospitals and will do almost anything to stay out of one; he was sure there were alternative options besides open-heart surgery. Needless to say, I didn't follow his advice.

Talk about bad timing – Mark had finally seen the benefit of a regular staff communications programme, and within a few weeks I was about to start work on the first ever edition of Lush TV. This time I was keeping the quirky formula I had developed for the training videos, but adding a modern handheld style that I felt suited the handmade nature of the business and could easily be combined with amateur footage sent in by Lush staff around the world.

In the October of 2006 we shot the first edition of Lush TV in a studio we had created in one of the rooms in the building that housed the Lush web team. It featured a raw brickwork background, a few large plants and an 'I Love Lush' light box borrowed from the Windows team. Rowena and Marco were to be the hosts but – typical of Lush – I wasn't told that Marco had left the company the day before the shoot and that Steve 'all things to everyone' had been volunteered to replace him.

It was too late to cancel and, with my operation two months away plus a three-month recovery period, there was no time to reschedule. I made up cue cards for Rowena and Steve, as we couldn't use autocue on a handheld camera. I didn't mind if they glanced at their cue cards now and then; it was all part of the deliberately rough style. I wanted it to feel like they had made it themselves albeit with high-quality pictures and sound.

The show contained features including the opening of the new Bournemouth shop, Lush Croatia's ten-year anniversary party, a charity bike ride for the Prince of Wales Trust (of which Mark had been a trustee), and various studio guests and topics. We also added the 'Steverella' pantomime performed by the newly formed Lush Players at the September managers' meeting as a special extra feature on the DVD. We replicated 650 DVDs in English to distribute to staff before Christmas.

There was no time to rest, as Mark had also commissioned *The History of Lush*, an illustrated long-form interview with him and Liz. We got the interview in the can but there were weeks of editing ahead to add all the archive material, and I now had other things on my mind.

I was scheduled for the last quadruple heart bypass of the year on Friday 15th December 2006. All being well, I'd be home for Christmas. Now, count backwards from ten... nine... eight... seven...

The first edtion of Lush TV presented by Rowena and Steve

# <u>13</u> PO Box Pelindaba

I had always felt that if I could find a living relative of John Constantine somewhere in Mark's family tree, I had a chance of finding the man himself. With just a month to go to Mark's sixtieth birthday, the discovery of Aunty June and the box of family photographs was the key to unlocking the mystery. There was still a massive gap between 1954 and 1964, and nothing at all after 1982, but with June's memories and her late mother's photograph collection I was now able to construct a timeline of the man I was looking for.

John Constantine had returned from Kenya around 1963 with a young woman, Prudence Marston Brogan (née Louis), who was eight years younger than him. She had been married and had a child in Kenya but was now separated from both her husband and the child, who was being raised by her parents. Following their respective divorces, John and Prudence were married in Stroud in March 1964. During this time they lived in Gloucestershire and John was working at the Berkeley nuclear power station. In 1966 John and Prudence had a baby daughter, Joanna, and two years later another baby girl, Sarie.

January 1969 saw the family board the SA Oranje at Southampton for a one-way passage to Cape Town. For the next twelve years John sent his mother occasional photographs of the girls growing up, although he never returned home, not even for his father's funeral in 1970.

Around 1980–82 John built a house somewhere in South Africa, but shortly after that the photographs stopped and the family in Manchester lost all communication with him. During the next few years they attempted to find him but had no luck, as he had only ever given them a PO Box number rather than his home address in South Africa. This seemed almost unbelievable, unless he wanted it that way. John had arrived in South Africa in January 1969, a forty-two-year-old man with a thirty-four-year-old wife and two baby daughters, and he was starting afresh. He had left behind his previous life, including the sixteen-year-old son he hadn't seen since he was a baby, his soon-to-die father, his mother and his adopted sister.

I spread out all the photographs in the order of the children growing up, looking for any clues and being careful to keep them with the actual envelopes in which they had been stored. There were no place names, and I could identify only the family arriving in Cape Town, and on a holiday there as soon as they disembarked. Crucially, one set of early photographs was still in the blue airmail envelope in which they had been sent. It had been torn open, and the postmark had barely survived, but under closer inspection I was able to read: 'PO BOX PELIN'. Out loud I cried 'Pelindaba!' as if I had won the lottery.

My first visit to South Africa had been in February 1996, two years after Nelson Mandela became president. I had directed filming at a steel plant in Pretoria, but on a weekend visit to Sun City the car journey had taken me over the Crocodile River on the road to the Hartbeespoort Dam, which passes a place called Pelindaba. A few years later I had been in South Africa again, this time filming a story about an electronic gases research project at a technology park in Pelindaba. During my visit I had learned that Pelindaba was the home of the South African Atomic Energy Corporation, where the South African government had developed atomic weapons between

1960 and 1980 before becoming the first country in the world to give up its nuclear armaments.

Now everything fell into place and I realised immediately that the industrial buildings I had spotted in the background of the last photograph John Constantine had sent home to his mother were the giant cooling towers of the power station. It was clear to me that John Constantine, a health physics monitor at a British nuclear power station during the late 1960s, had applied to join the South African nuclear programme, and had emigrated with his family to Pelindaba in 1969.

I searched for the location on Google Maps and brought up an aerial view. From my previous trips I remembered crossing the bridge over the Crocodile River on the R104 from Pretoria, and the junction with Pelindaba Road just beyond it. Somewhere up there on the escarpment overlooking the place where he worked was the home of John Constantine. Even if he wasn't still living there, I was pretty sure I could find him – or, if he had died, his daughters.

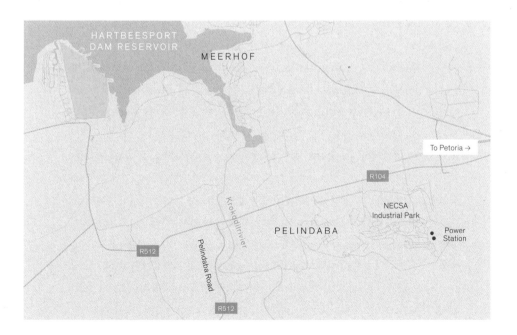

A quick search online provided the website of the South African Nuclear Energy Corporation (now called NECSA, a research facility for nuclear energy and technology projects). I wondered if it had a retirement association and so trawled their website until I spotted something called the pensioners forum. Here I found a Christmas 2011 newsletter and pictures of the NECSA pensioners' party. I had no idea what an eighty-three-year-old John Constantine would look like or if he was even a member, but I did find the name of the secretary of the association who was thanked by the chairman in his annual speech. Her name was Petra Grundling and I sent her an email via the NECSA contact webmail address. I informed her that I was an amateur genealogist trying to track down a relative of a family in the UK who had lost contact with him in 1982 and wanted to know if he was still alive. I said that he had joined the company in January 1969 and if it was permissible for her to help, I would supply his name.

I could not be sure if the email would reach her and I had already come to the judgement that Mark should make the final decision as to whether or not to pursue the search to the very end, but I had done all I could. Now it was a race to get all the family history collated and I simply had to fly up to Manchester to meet Aunty June.

June and her daughter Bernadette made me feel very welcome in the small Constantine family home in Little Hulton, where I knew that John had lived and had gone to the local grammar school. They showed me his school report which confirmed that he been a very bright pupil. Also in their possession was an old family photograph from around 1900. They were not sure who was pictured but I knew straight away: it was the cabinetmaker Thomas Henry Constantine, his wife Elizabeth and their six children including Mark's grandfather John Hyde sitting on his father's knee. It was pure gold, a family portrait of Mark's great grandparents, which I dated to 1907.

I showed June and Bernadette the DVD of Mark and Mo's OBE presentation, and photographs of him and his family. They had no

1907, TYLDESLEY, LANCASHIRE

Mark's great grandfather Thomas with grandfather John Hyde on his knee

idea that the founder of Lush, now a highly successful British businessman, was their nephew and cousin. Once again, June said they
had presumed many, many years ago that Mark had taken the name
of his stepfather and so had not grown up as a Constantine.

With my time in Manchester restricted to a few hours, I outlined
how I was planning a birthday dinner for Mark and Mo at my house
on the eve of his birthday, during which I would present him with his
family history. I added that I intended to give him the information
in the order that I had found it, so that he could experience the
unravelling of his family history in the same way I had.

June was both excited and nervous, and I promised to phone

her when it was over to tell her how it went. Bernadette took a lovely picture of June and me in the back garden, and I took some photographs of the house and the memorial plaque from the grave of Mark's grandparents that June had rescued from the local cemetery and placed in her garden among the gnomes.

On the flight back to Southampton I reflected on all that I had learned from talking to June, and concluded that John Constantine could never have remained in Manchester. Born to working-class parents, in the heart of the industrial North, he excelled at grammar school and was never going to follow his father down the mines. Instead he chose adventurous careers in the RAF, the London Met, the Royal Kenyan Police and finally the secret world of atomic bombs in Pelindaba, South Africa.

Pelindaba was originally a farm owned by the South African historian and writer Gustav Preller. He named it by combining two Zulu words, 'phela' and 'ndaba.' Together they mean 'the end of business' or 'the conclusion.' I was now very close to the end of my search for Mark's father.

2012, LITTLE HULTON, MANCHESTER

Aunty June and me, in the garden of the Constantine family home

# <u>14</u> Mark, Me & Lush TV

In February 2007, just eight weeks after my heart-bypass operation, we started filming edition two of Lush TV. Our featured shop was Glasgow Buchannan Street whose manager had won the Christmas Queen award for highest sales during the 2006 Christmas season. They staged a Valentine's Day special with all the staff in romantic or sexy costumes. We were filming a sequence with a sales assistant in a tantalising basque when a scruffy-looking guy walked in off the street I thought he was drunk and we'd have to ask him to leave, but at that very moment he walked up to the counter and bought the most expensive Lush Legends gift box for £99.99. Never judge a book by its cover!

The programme also featured the first of many campaign films, where Andrew Butler, Lush's new campaigns manager, tried to dump tons of manure on the steps of the EU Parliament in Strasbourg as a protest against the EU failing to ratify its legislation banning the testing of cosmetics on animals. In addition, Simon Constantine had just returned from Indonesia with a story about the palm-oil industry and how deforestation was causing major problems for the indigenous orangutan population.

In the studio, Rowena introduced Ruth Andrade, a Brazilian environmentalist whom Mark had recruited to lead Lush's environmental policies. Ruth was and still is a very passionate and inspiring campaigner with whom I would make many 'green' features for

Lush TV. I think Mark saw a lot of Anita in Ruth – she has that same infectious, can-do personality, and you only have to point a camera at her and she will turn you into an eco-warrior in a few minutes. Mark gave her carte blanche to make the Lush organisation as green as possible, from reducing their carbon footprint to mini-mising packaging, by now a key Lush policy. Mark had yet to make an appearance on Lush TV, but he did devote a week to making a documentary, *Packaging is Rubbish*, for Channel 4.

By July 2007 we had reached edition three and the show was positively packed with features – the opening of the Moscow European Mall shop and other new shops in Turkey and the USA, an ylang ylang buying trip to the Comoros Islands, a shea butter buying trip to Ghana, and Lush's naked campaign – all of which dovetailed nicely with the airing of Mark's documentary. To draw attention to the minimal and often naked packaging of Lush's products, staff volunteered to go naked for a day, wearing only their aprons to cover their modesty. We shot the Lush TV feature in Carnaby Street, with the staff posing for the press in front of the shop before turn-ing round to reveal their naked bottoms. As one of the Lush girls sashayed up the street for the cameras, a passer-by literally walked into a lamppost! (In 2018 Lush opened its first 'naked shop' in Milan, where all the products have no packaging).

Ask me why I'm Naked campaign

Whenever I spoke to Mark around that time, the topic was always the phenom-enal growth of Lush Japan, which, to a large extent, was driving the profits of the business. Shops were being opened in Japan at an astonishing rate, far outnumbering the growth in the UK. Products were invented specifically for the Japanese market to tie in with cultural differences such as White Day on the 14th March, their equivalent of Valentine's Day, when the tradition is for women to give gifts to men. A young Japanese woman, Noriko, was a permanent member of the Poole lab team, working very closely with Mo and Helen, and with her help we added Japanese subtitles to Lush TV for the benefit of the hundreds of employees in Lush Japan.

If all this makes it sound like Lush TV was a slick operation, nothing could be further from the truth. There wasn't yet sufficient budget to send me overseas to film reports, so much of the material coming in was shot by staff, with varying levels of competence. We had, however, reached three editions in a row without Mark cancelling or revamping the project in some way, which in itself was grounds for optimism, and the handheld style was proving a successful way of combining professional and amateur footage to make a regular internal communications programme to which staff could relate. It had to reflect both the ethics and fun of working for Lush while also making staff feel part of a global community; it was a TV show by Lush people for Lush people.

On 10th September 2007 Dame Anita Roddick died at the age of sixty-four. She suffered a major brain haemorrhage at St Richard's Hospital in Chichester, West Sussex. Mark found out late in the day and took the phone off the hook so that he didn't have to talk to anyone. He had been very critical of Anita's decision to sell The Body Shop and now wished he hadn't been so outspoken. He told me that he woke up around 4am the following morning and wrote a piece about how he felt about Anita; it was an outpouring of love for a woman who had found him wandering in the wilderness in 1976 and shown him the way to follow his dreams and make his fortune. Just writing about Anita helped Mark to make sense of why she sold the business, but still not why she sold it to L'Oreal, who, in his eyes, was the antithesis of ethical cosmetics. She could have sold it to Mark. Lush did offer £450 million at one point, but I thought that was Mark just chancing his arm. How he would have successfully absorbed 2000 Body Shops into the Lush organisation immediately prior to the banking crisis is hard to envisage. It would have been a decision of the heart more than the head. Mark cared deeply for The Body Shop and, when Anita died prematurely, Mark felt that her dream had died with her.

There is no doubt that Mark revered Anita and throughout his life there is a pattern of respect for strong women stretching back to his grandmother. Perhaps being brought up in a women only house for most of his childhood, gave him a better understanding of the female psyche, as I could write a very long list of the talented women with whom he has worked and promoted through his business. In its own way, it's a tribute to his Nan.

During this period of mourning for arguably Britain's greatest female entrepreneur, Lush continued to grow and now had 462 shops trading in thirty-nine countries from South Korea to Chile, Estonia to Saudi Arabia, and global sales of £116 million. Mark left most of the international start-ups to Rowena. She had her own ROW team (Rest of the World), which was anywhere that wasn't North America, the EU, Japan or Australia, and she often brought back great stories for Lush TV.

In November 2007 Lush TV edition four went out, containing our now-regular feature of a factory tour and a song at the end of the show. This year it was Christmas gifts and, led by Rowena, the gifts-manufacturing team were happy to don elf hats and sing a festive song for the camera, even if the first language of most of them was Polish or Arabic. Lush is well known – and even publicly crit- icised by some – for employing large numbers of EU migrants and refugees, especially over the busy Christmas period from September to January. People jump to the conclusion that this is in order to take advantage of cheap labour, but in fact everyone is paid the same rate at Lush whether they are local British employees or international workers. Same pay scale, same bonus. In truth, Lush has a problem recruiting enough local staff to man its factories in the Poole area, where they have probably employed more school-leavers than any other business in Dorset.

Lush has an open-borders policy and Mark is staunchly pro-European. As the head of a company that has shops and factories in close to fifty countries, with staff speaking forty-odd languages, how could he be otherwise? Mark himself does not speak any other language – apart from a little scientific Latin, the long-established international language of birdwatchers, botanists and all who work in the field of natural sciences – but he speaks in English and often for a very long time if you are filming him and looking for just a snappy soundbite.

The subjects Mark is most passionate about are environmental protection, human rights, and animal welfare – as reflected in his lifelong effort to end the use of animal testing in the cosmetics industry. Yes, he is a capitalist but one with a conscience and the means to do something about issues

2008, LUSH REGENT STREET, LONDON

Fair Trial My Arse campaign supported by Bill Bailey and Kevin Eldon

that he feels are unjust. He often allows his shops to be used by campaigning groups to help them get their messages to the public.

The 'Fair Trial My Arse' campaign was one of the most powerful of all the Lush campaigns, directed at freeing the Al Jazeera cameraman Sami al-Hajj and other wrongfully arrested detainees at Guantanamo Bay. Lush employees wore bright orange knickers (the colour of the overalls worn by Guantanamo detainees) and asked customers to sign a petition in support of Reprieve, the organisation headed by the human-rights lawyer Clive Stafford-Smith. Mo created a special bath bomb that fizzed away to release a picture of Sami and other detainees whom Reprieve were actively trying to get released. As Mo commented at the time, it was the point where a simple bath product became a way to help save lives. Sami, a journalist, was arrested in Afghanistan in 2001 just doing his job, and detained without a fair trial until May 2008. After his release, he came and thanked Lush staff – which of course we captured for Lush TV.

In another prominent campaign, Alice Newstead, a member of staff at Lush was suspended in the Regent Street shop window by large shark fishing hooks pierced through her skin in order to highlight the inhumane practice of shark finning. Every year, tens of millions of sharks die a horribly slow death because of finning, which involves the shark's fins being hacked off and its living body thrown back into the sea. Shark fins are harvested to supply the growing demand for shark-fin soup, an Asian delicacy. Mark could not bear to watch the campaign video that we made for Lush TV; it was too graphic and hard-hitting.

The palm oil campaign was promoted constantly, both in the UK and across the Lush world, where customers were encouraged to put their palm prints on the shop windows in support of the Orang-Rimba indigenous people of Indonesia, and the native orangutans. Both are being displaced by the relentless slashing and burning of natural forest in order to create space for vast areas of palm oil plantations. Lush have replaced palm oil in the production of their soaps. They were also early advocates of using natural, biodegradable alternatives to microbeads, the tiny plastic pellets in cosmetics, which are causing great harm to the oceans and marine wildlife.

In 2008, Lush Japan reached the milestone of opening a hundred shops, which prompted resident Lush musician Simon Nicholls to celebrate with a song based on a reworking of The Proclaimers' *I'm Gonna Be (500 Miles)*. We persuaded the board of directors to sing the song on Lush TV: 'And we will open one hundred shops And we will open one hundred more ...'

There seemed to be no stopping Lush Japan, which boasted sales of £45 million in 2008 and regularly had the highest-grossing shops in terms of turnover, in the world. Each year four or five of the top-ten global shops would be in Japan, one a tiny store based in Tokyo's busiest subway station. I was itching to go out there and film the Japanese business, but the nation that invented the camcorder kept doing it for me.

Back in the UK, Mark had decided to rebrand Lush, going for a more contemporary high-street look. Lush has always had a very strong design team, headed by Jo Evans and Katie Tabram, and in the autumn of 2008 they unveiled the new-look Lush store with the rebranding of the Kingston shop,

2008, LUSH KINGSTON-UPON-THAMES
New look, Lush shop interior

one of the original Lush shops from 1997. Gone was the green logo, replaced by the plain LUSH, along with a natural wood look to the shop interiors and sinks fitted to make shop demonstrations easier for staff. That's a very succinct description of the move away from green and yellow, which took years to achieve, but it was the start of the process, that has evolved into the modern look of Lush on the high street today. Lush Kingston became the flagship store and we used it often for filming Lush TV and making product demonstration videos for the Lush TV YouTube channel.

During this three-year period Mark had been supporting Rowena's dream to add make-up products to the brand, although it did not fit easily into the Lush concept, as lipsticks, eye shadows and blushers required a certain amount of protective and application packaging. They got around this by opening a sister brand, B Never Too Busy To Be Beautiful, which was a bit of a mouthful but came in the form of half a dozen shops usually sited next door to a popular Lush shop. Apart from having the same ethics, 'B' was all glamour and glitz and everything that Lush wasn't, and Rowena was very much its public face. We even had a regular 'B spot' on Lush TV, for the growing numbers of 'B' staff, and Rowena opened a shop in Tokyo to great fanfare.

It was another example of Mark's mischievous side – to take a punt and see what came from rolling the dice in the beauty world – and reached a climax with the opening of a 1,500-square foot 'B' shop on Oxford Street in early 2009. The opening night featured celebrity guests just like *Hello!* magazine, and striking young women in black cocktail dresses. These were the 'B' sales assistants and make-up artists. I bumped into Mark's fellow director Andrew in the basement. 'How much does this shop cost Andrew?' I casually enquired. 'Let's just say we need to take £500,000 a year just to pay the rent,' he replied with a raised eyebrow.

I can't understand why Mark ventured into the high-stakes world of beauty, taking on the likes of Rimmel and Max Factor, when Lush was growing steadily as a high-street

2009, OXFORD STREET, LONDON
'B' opening day

cosmetics brand and had just opened a large new-look store in the Westfield shopping mall in White City. Mark did start his career with Elizabeth Arden in Bond Street and maybe, when the opportunity presented itself, he just couldn't resist it. All entrepreneurs have their mad moments; in fact, it's probably a compulsory trait.

The 'B' experiment was closed when it became clear that the Oxford Street shop was a massive black hole, but the lessons learned eventually enabled Lush to introduce a make-up and colour cosmetics range into their stores albeit in a simpler way that complemented the other products in the brand. It also demonstrated that Mark has no fear of taking bold decisions, and he was about to hand me another mission impossible.

In early 2009, Lush played host to the BBC show *The Apprentice*, where the apprentices were let loose in the Poole factory to create a new cosmetic product to be judged by their would-be boss, Sir Alan now Lord Sugar. The Lush manufacturing team gave them every assistance, although they were all sworn to secrecy until the show aired. They were not allowed to have a copy of the film or use *The Apprentice* brand to promote Lush in any way. Try telling that to Mark!

Mo invented a sugar-scrub skin exfoliator to go on sale in the shops the day after the Lush edition of *The Apprentice* aired. It even featured a cartoon illustration of Sir Alan Sugar, and the strapline was another one of Mo's clever play on words: 'Sugar has never been this good for your figure.' The next day Mark got a call from Sir Alan telling him in no uncertain terms to remove the product or be sued. Mark tried to assuage the highly successful British businessman by saying that it was just a bit of fun and a way of getting some publicity for all the help Lush had given him. Sir Alan pointed out that Lush had not helped him personally, only the TV production company. Mark agreed to remove the product, but it took a couple of days.

However, Lush's involvement with the show gave Karl a great idea. The next managers' meeting was just a few weeks away and Karl persuaded Mark to hold his own version of *The Apprentice*; to divide all his managers into teams and challenge them to come up with a new product in two days. I was tasked to film a special feature for Lush TV called '*Ready, Steady, Create*.' As so often happens with Lush, small ideas get bigger: the original plan of five teams working in two factories became ten teams in six locations – quite a logistical challenge and so I drafted in some film-school students on work experience to supplement my regular crews.

The Lush teams all had to visit key locations for their fragrances, essential ingredients, label design and the production process. Over two days of intensive and often frantic filming, we captured the key manufacturing sequence of the winning team who came up with a spot cleanser called Grease Lightning, which eventually went into the shops and became a hot favourite with teenagers.

By 2009 Mark's twenty-five-year-old son Jack was heading up the Lush web team and he had lots of ideas for using video to establish a presence on YouTube. He brought in one of his schoolmates, Henry Dalton, a film-school graduate, to create web videos including a trilogy called 'Lush Town.' It was a spoof detective story, similar to the video Mark and I had made for The Body Shop twenty years earlier, and Mark needed no persuading to play the elusive Mr Big who rescues the heroine and winks at the camera in the final shot.

Mark's elder son, Simon, was now an up-and-coming perfumer and had just released a perfume called 'Breath of God' inspired by his travels in the Himalayas. It got a five-star rating in *Perfumes: The A to Z Guide*, the definitive critique of all the perfume brands including the likes of Channel and Dior; something his father had yet to achieve. They now share a lab in 29 High Street, where there is a large perfumer's organ – a rack containing a small bottle of every essential oil and botanical fragrance found on earth, not something you play a tune on. Meanwhile, nineteen-year-old Claire was about to start her apprenticeship at Lush on the retail side of the business, and just for fun Mark and I invested £4000 each in a London indie rock band in which my younger son Michael, was the drummer. It never made us any money but it did help

2014, 29 HIGH STREET, POOLE
Mark and his perfumer's organ

them to get noticed and in due course signed by a record label.

The big news of 2009, aside from adding Russian subtitles to Lush TV, was undoubtedly the opening of the Lush Spa on the Kings Road, another one of Mark's big ideas, which featured a Synaesthesia treatment at the heart of the spa experience. In many ways the Lush Spa is a project of huge self-indulgence, bringing together all the things Mark likes in one place: music, bird sounds, poetry, essential oils, and relaxation therapies. However, it's not like a conventional spa; the massage is choreographed to music, like a ballet, and you are transported into different worlds depending on your choice of treatment. The original Synaesthesia treatment uses the stimulation of one sense to create a sensation felt elsewhere in the body. It was developed by Mark's behavioural hypnotherapist, Lady Helen Kennedy, one of a select number of alternative practitioners that Mark and Mo have turned to over the years in preference to conventional medicine. Lady Helen told Mark that if he gave someone a body treatment that opened their mind, he would create a treatment second to none. She helped him associate certain emotions with smells and sounds, like the dawn chorus or the lapping of waves on the shoreline.

For the music, Mark turned to the Bridport-based composer and musician Simon Emmerson, who coincidentally is a birder himself.

2009, KINGS ROAD, LONDON
The first Lush Spa

Mark met him through the Dorset Bird Club and watched him perform a gig with his band, Imagined Village. Mark was so taken with the music that he persuaded Simon to write and produce the score for the Synaesthesia treatment and eight other treatments that have been developed since. Simon is now the Lush music director, and he and Mark have their own record label, ECC (Emmerson, Corncrake and Constantine), which has released CDs of all the Spa music as well as vinyl albums of the many musicians Simon has introduced to Lush including the world-renowned sitarist Sheema Mukherjee.

Lush TV was now being distributed to 8,000 worldwide employees in English, Japanese and Russian, all on one menu-driven DVD, which added twenty working days from the final studio recording day with Rowena and Steve, to delivery to the Lush warehouse. After that, there were also shipping times to the various Lush countries,

2013, LIVERPOOL LUSH SPA LAUNCH

Sheema Mukherjee & Simon Emmerson

meaning it was never very current when it reached its audience, which is why we always filmed the Christmas edition in September. Each year the Lush Christmas range was showcased to the UK and international managers at a massive gathering in London in September. It was a great opportunity to get the end-of-year edition of Lush TV shot and distributed before Christmas, so at least one edition was actually current at the time of release.

Mark and the founders were often the centre of attention at these events, where staff queued up to have their photograph taken with them, particularly the Japanese who revered the founders almost like gods. The event had now moved to a large country hotel near Croydon, and the grounds were used by the Lush Players to stage little playlets based around the inspiration for the products. The managers were divided into groups and literally walked through the woods from one setting to another where they would be treated to a ten-minute show and demonstrations of products like Snow Fairy or Satsumo Santa, a bubble bath that smelled of satsuma oranges with a Japanese twist. Steve 'all things to everyone' Brackstone played Satsumo Santa, one of his many hilarious characters.

The event was also used to stage a charity auction where huge amounts of money was raised to fund various small charities supported by Lush. It often went on into the small hours with Mark, Andrew Gerrie and the Lush North America CEO Mark Wolverton bidding outrageous amounts for silly items. Even after this, they would double the amount raised at the end of the evening.

We were all inspired by a talk from Lamin Daffeh, who ran a charity called the Fresh Start Foundation in the Gambia that aimed to provide primary school education and school meals for orphans and other vulnerable children. Lamin had tried to win money for his charity on Noel Edmonds' TV show *Deal or No Deal* but lost everything on the last call. He came away from the Lush charity auction with £8,000, which Mark doubled to £16,000 out of his own pocket.

All of these events and stories went into Lush TV plus a new feature called 'The Mark and Andrew Business Update.' I never knew what they were going to talk about when they sat down in front of the camera and I'm not sure they did either, but at least we had reached ten editions of Lush TV without me coming to blows with Mark.

The February 2010 edition of Lush TV was a cracker as Rowena and Steve had got together a group of Lush volunteers to go to the Gambia to help Lamin rebuild a school, and my cameraman Chris Bowerman volunteered to go with them and filmed an inspiring story. We also had 'The Hunts Are Still At It' campaign, devoted to Lush's long-standing support of the Hunt Saboteurs Association. The Blair government had passed a law banning the hunting of foxes with hounds, but the ban was being flagrantly ignored by some hunts.

Of all the activist groups that Mark and Lush have supported down the years, his support of the Hunt Saboteurs has brought him some of the most adverse publicity. His shop staff have been threatened by pro-hunt supporters, displays in the shops have been deliberately knocked over, and the Countryside Alliance has tried to paint Mark as a millionaire who backs a violent group of extremists. When Mark's house was broken into early in 2010 and just a laptop, camera and memory sticks were taken – he was genuinely convinced that he was being targeted, and possibly even covertly investigated as a 'domestic extremist.' He didn't have any proof of this so his response was to present a film about what he saw as illogical policing funding priorities for the BBC's *Daily Politics* show. He demonstrated how the police's National Wildlife Crime Unit were so underfunded that they could not enforce the new fox-hunting law, and that the hunt saboteurs had been forced to come out of retirement and do it themselves.

Mark was also accused of funding the group Plane Stupid so that they could chain themselves to airport runways and stop flights. Lush did give them a small amount of money, but they don't decide the tactics of Plane Stupid. In order to lower the company's carbon footprint Mark does not generally allow his staff to fly anywhere in the UK, while he and other Lush staff always fly economy on business trips abroad.

2010, LUSH KINGS ROAD, LONDON
The Hunts Are Still At It! Campaign

He supports Brian May and the Save Me campaign to stop the badger cull in the UK, and has worked closely with Clive Stafford-Smith of Reprieve to right human injustices around the world. When I say he, it's actually the whole Lush organisation that gets behind these issues, which are different in every country – for example, the Tar Sands campaign in North America or the anti-bullfighting campaign in Spain.

The right wing press in the UK often label Mark as a 'Corbynista' and while he has invited Jeremy Corbyn and John McDonnell to speak to his staff at Lush summits, he is first and foremost an environmentalist and a long time patron of Caroline Lucas MP of the Green Party.

More recently government ministers and even the Home Secretary have publicly criticised Lush for supporting the campaign group Police Spies Out Of Lives, accusing the company of irresponsible and dangerous behaviour. The truth is that for 50 years over 1000 campaign groups including environmental campaigners, trade unions and even justice groups like the Stephen Lawrence family campaign, have been spied on by at least 250 undercover police officers. These so called 'spy cops' were paid to infiltrate peoples' lives including their homes and beds, and a number of women were tricked into long-term relationships, causing them great emotional distress when they discovered the truth. Mark is passionate about supporting these honest women and other citizens who stand up for perfectly legal principled action and have the right to be heard.

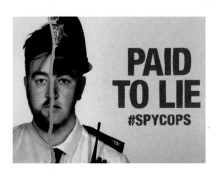

2018, LUSH OXFORD STREET
The first SpyCops campaign window

Although Mark himself is a generous individual donor, most of the money is raised through the Lush Charity Pot. It's managed by Lush's ethics director, Hilary Jones, and Lush's head of charitable giving, Rebecca Lush, herself a famous activist who once slapped a custard pie in Jeremy Clarkson's face and was arrested during the construction of the M3 through Twyford Down in Hampshire. I have worked with Hilary, Rebecca and many others at Lush who passionately believe you can have both a commercial business and one that cares about the environment and human rights. Who else but a Lush employee would dress up as an endangered orangutan and be strapped to a spinning circus wheel while knives were thrown at them? I kid you not; I have the film to prove it.

The *Lush Go To Gambia* documentary proved to be a landmark film that set the standard of Lush TV for years to follow, and we moved the presentation of the show into a shop for the first time. From this point on, Lush TV came from a real location not a studio set, and in the summer we found ourselves live at Lushfest 2010, an event for staff held in a large marquee outside the main factories in Poole. Various charities supported by Lush had stands in the tents, and all the manufacturing teams showed off their side of the business. It culminated with Mark leading the last leg of the Lush charity cycle relay, which had started at Lush Inverness and passed through many Lush shops in the country before ending in Poole. It was done to raise awareness of cycle lanes and the benefits of cycling – a campaign that harked back to Mark's Friends of the Earth days in the early 1970s.

A big feature of the show was the launch of the new 'Tuca Tuca' fragrance, with Lush's resident pop singer Mira Livingston, aka Mira Manga, performing both the song and the accompanying dance on stage in the tent. Mark had been to a managers' meeting in Lush Italy when he was introduced to this bizarre Italian song and dance from the 1950s. It had inspired him to create a violet-scented fragrance as part of a collection of perfumes that he and Simon were about to launch in London.

The Gorilla Perfume Gallery, held in the old town hall in Shoreditch, showcased Lush's new range of perfumes. This was another big project on the scale of the Lush Spa. Mark and Simon had originally chosen to call them themselves Guerilla Perfumers, a sort of anti-establishment poke at mainstream perfumers whose products were all overpriced and overpackaged, but allegedly when Jack Constantine heard the name he jokingly suggested it ought to be Gorilla, a reference to his older brother's large physique. True or not, the name stuck, as did the banana logo; only Mark would have the impertinence to take on the perfume market with such a ridiculous brand name.

The perfume gallery, designed by Jo and Katie, was a design tour de force with every nook and cranny of the basement arts centre taken up with a visual story about each perfume. Lust was a young woman's clothes-strewn bedroom, Tuca Tuca was a dance floor with actual dancers; Dirty was a men's toilet in a nightclub. A special

Simon Constantine outside
the first Gorilla gallery

limited collection, named the Heiress, the
Duchess and the Actress, was based on
three women who Mark met at the Elizabeth Arden salon in 1972 when he was a
twenty-year-old hairdresser. The resulting
Lush TV feature was a very special one;
the first time Mark had made a film with
his son and the first time I had done the
same, as much of the soundtrack featured
East London indie rock music courtesy of
my son's band Life in Film.

At Mark and Mo's annual New
Year's Eve party that year, they informed us
they had been awarded OBEs for their contribution to the UK beauty
industry and named in the New Year Honours List. There was even
a pretty impressive royal parchment from the Queen (which Mark
and Mo's grandchildren accidently used as colouring paper the next
day). To celebrate Mark and Mo's investiture by the Queen herself
on 6th May 2011, Lush brought out a bath bomb in the shape of an
OBE. Naturally this was a huge story for Lush TV and we filmed
a special feature at the Lush Windsor shop,
where the staff wore tiaras in their hair and
demonstrated the OBE bath bomb; it was
all great fun. Although we weren't allowed
in the castle itself, we filmed the Changing of the Guard ceremony with the band
marching through the streets, and captured
Mark and Mo as they emerged from Windsor
Castle gate with their proud children. There
was a celebratory lunch for family and close
friends at Heston Blumenthal's restaurant in
Bray. All were there except, of course, Mark's

New Year's Eve

father John Constantine, now presumed lost forever.

Later that summer Geri and I took Mark and Mo back to Weymouth to open the Rose Queen Festival at St Edmund's Church, which we had both attended as boys and where we had strutted the stage with the St Edmund's Players. They really enjoyed themselves and Mark got to meet some people from his teenage years, including the girl in the choir whom he'd had a crush on but never dated.

Soon, we were all preparing for the biggest Lush event ever. After the success of the mini Lushfest in 2010, Mark decided to host a much bigger event in 2011, where managers and staff from around the world could be immersed in all things Lush. There was now so much to show off and talk about that a two-day meeting followed by a two-day music and culture festival seemed like a great way to inspire the entire global Lush organisation, which now operated in over forty countries and had global sales approaching £300 million.

After much searching, a location was found on the Holton Lee estate, near Wareham. It was already a well-being centre with lovely walks and harbour views, and plenty of fields in which to accommodate a festival site and an adjoining camping area. Simon Emmerson arranged most of the music programme, each factory manufacturing team had their own area, and many of the Lush charities and action groups were invited to show off their work. There was a funfair, a pub, any number of food tents, and a massive campsite of tents for the 1,500-plus staff attending from around the world.

The summer edition of Lush TV was scheduled to be produced live at the festival, and we planned to shoot and edit on site all the various musicians, bands and events during the two-day festival before uploading them to the Lush YouTube channel. It was a huge undertaking requiring multiple camera crews and on-site vision mixing and editing.

On the main stage the opening act was Simon Emmerson's

Mark and Mo with their OBEs at Windsor Castle

Afro Celt Sound System, a multicultural band that play a fusion of traditional Irish and West African music. I stood out front with Mark, watching it on the big screen as a camera mounted on a Jimmy Jib crane swung across the packed tent to capture amazing pictures of the band and the enthusiastic crowd. It was one of the highlights of my career, and the edited version of the show was just a joy to direct: I had shot some time-lapse sequences, which enabled me to end the documentary style of Lush TV with the fields of Holton Lee returning back to nature after the festival had departed the site, and for good luck I included one of Mark's dawn-chorus bird recordings as a soundtrack. He said it was the best Lush TV ever and that in future all of them needed to be to this standard. Hmmm!

The year held one more surprise, when Mark asked me to produce a Christmas video for the website. Simon Emmerson had produced a folksy version of Slade's *Merry Christmas Everybody.* He put together a band and I got permission from the council to film them busking outside the Bournemouth shop. The town was already

2012, HOLTON LEE, WAREHAM, DORSET
The Lush Players at Lushfest

lit for Christmas, there was a funfair in the square, and the Lush shop was dressed in the Christmas theme of Willy Wonka. Lush staff came down in their Christmas pullovers to form a crowd, although a passing stag party in fancy dress added extra realism. Steve dressed up as a drunk Santa from an office party being helped home by two girls, and we shot the whole thing at night on new digital cameras.

In April 2012 Lush embarked on perhaps its most controversial campaign to date. Within the EU there was already a ban on the testing of cosmetic ingredients on animals – irrespective of whether there were non-animal alternatives. It had also banned the testing of cosmetic products in the EU. However, this didn't apply to countries outside the EU, so cosmetic manufacturers in the EU could get around the ban by testing in other countries. In 2012, there was a big push by Humane Society International, with their Be Cruelty Free campaign, to bring this issue to a head and force the EU to implement a total ban. Lush staff from all over Europe, dressed as rabbits, staged a flash dance outside the EU Commission in Brussels to publicise the huge public petition that was being delivered by Humane Society International.

To launch the petition in the UK, Lush's new campaigns

manager, Tamsin Omond, came up with a PR stunt to test on a human, in the same way as is done with animals, in a mock laboratory set up in the window of Lush Regent Street. A performance artiste was hired to have liquid squirted into her eyes and endure other gruesome tests, such as force-feeding, by a white-coated lab technician. She was even dragged into the window on a collar and chain. She remained in the window throughout the day, with the lab coated technician regularly returning to conduct the next experiment, which drew large crowds and plenty of press photographers. At the end of the day, Hilary had the brilliant idea of carrying the 'dead' actor out into the street and dumping her body in the gutter with the rubbish. Lush TV was the only TV crew covering the event and I knew that we had PR gold in our hands.

2012, EU COMMISSION, BRUSSELS

Lush Europe staff flash dancing to publicise the delivery of the petition

Testing cosmetics on a human in the shop window in support
of Humane Society International

We worked through the night to edit the YouTube video and supply clips to the BBC, as Tamsin was due to appear on *BBC Breakfast* the following morning. In the end they didn't use our clips as they were deemed too graphic, but once on YouTube the video went viral. It was the culmination of years of campaigning on this issue by Mark and his colleagues at Lush, and in March the following year the EU completed the ban on selling cosmetics in Europe that have been tested on animals anywhere in the world. The ban applies to both cosmetic products and ingredients. I rate the YouTube video as the best piece of work I have produced for Mark because it was such an effective short film that really made people sit up and take notice. It's had millions of views, way more than any other film I have ever made, and you can still watch it on YouTube.

On a lighter note, in early July the Lush TV cameras were rolling for a local celebrity, as Margaret Constantine OBE was invited to run a leg of the Olympic torch relay in Poole.

2012, UPTON, POOLE

Official photograph of Mo carrying
the Olympic torch

# <u>15</u> 'Sawubona'

July 21st 2012, Mark's sixtieth birthday, had loomed large on my calendar for nine months. I still didn't know whether I would find eighty-three-year-old John Constantine dead or alive. I was so close that I was tempted to jump on a plane to South Africa, but that wasn't possible because the first two weeks of July were taken up with Lushfest 2012.

The 2011 Lushfest had been a great success but attendance had been limited to Lush staff and there had been just one main stage. The 2012 event was going to be much bigger and bolder, with two main music stages and other smaller music and performance venues, and the Lush-loving public allowed to buy tickets. This one really was like Glastonbury on a smaller scale, and big enough to cost the company several million pounds. It required five TV crews and eighteen staff just to manage the live TV coverage, which this year was being shown on large screens around the venue as well as being edited on site and fed to YouTube. We had requisitioned one of the few buildings on site as our HQ.

Lushfest 2012 was another example of Mark's propensity for pushing an idea to its absolute limits. Doubling the size and inviting the public to the weekend festivities brought considerable logistical challenges, the successful managing of which would depend greatly on having good weather.

2012, HOLTON LEE, WAREHAM, DORSET

Simon Constantine launching the Set in Stone perfume range in the
stone circle at Lushfest

Although it was raining hard when staff started to arrive on
the campsite, people had brought their wellington boots and were
in good spirits. We even had a brief respite on the second evening
of the staff event, when a glorious sunset provided the perfect
setting for Simon to launch his new perfume range called Set in
Stone. Inspired by the many ancient stone circles in Dorset and
Wiltshire, combined with the nature of the English countryside
and the indigenous plants that grew around these ancient sites,
Simon had come up with a collection of perfumes with intriguing names like The Devil's Nightcap and Flowers Barrow. The big
surprise was a modern-day stone circle, built by Lush in a quiet

corner of the Lushfest site. Individual stones were doused in the scent of the various fragrances, and people were invited to go around sniffing the stones while the composer John Metcalfe played live music from a specially commissioned orchestral piece that he had co-written with Simon Richmond. It was truly inspired and moving. The Set in Stone vinyl album was later released by ECC Records and forms part of the ECC 100 collection that you can listen to and buy in Lush shops.

The Set in Stone evening was the only ray of sunshine at Lushfest 2012 and the next few days brought the wettest week in a hundred years, with whole villages in Dorset cut off. The festival site quickly became a quagmire and the grass car parks unusable by anything less than a 4x4. A grim-faced Mark came into the TV studio on the Saturday morning, the driest place on site, to make the weighty decision of whether or not to cancel the weekend music festival. The public could not drive onto the site, which was only reachable via a single track lane, but Mark decided to go ahead and gave Steve 'all things to everyone' the job of organising some form of park and ride for those members of the public who had bought tickets. Steve was one of my two Lush TV presenters but, with his hands full saving the festival, Rowena had to present the show largely on her own.

It rained pretty much non-stop throughout Saturday and Sunday, and keeping the electrical and TV equipment dry was a major headache, but we ploughed on, united by a do-or-die festival spirit. My favourite piece was a song by an American folk singer called Wooden Wand, who sang about living in a shack with a leaky roof, and my cameraman got a great backlit shot of rain dripping into the tent where he was playing his set.

Throughout all this, I was carrying the knowledge that I had found Aunty June, precious family photographs including some of Mark as a child, and the last known location of his father and sisters. Every time I bumped into Mark on site I felt a slight sense of guilt that I knew more about his family history than he did, but there was only a couple of weeks to go until his birthday.

Much of that was taken up editing the Lushfest edition of Lush TV, a DVD now in four languages that we sent to 10,000 members of staff around the world. However, I spent every spare minute writing up the history of both the Constantine and Gardner families based on what I knew to be true and confirmed by all the birth, marriage and death certificates I had collected and the census returns, war records, and ship's passenger lists.

I bound Mark's family history into a suede leather binder and made up a gift box containing all the photographs Aunty June had given me. And to my delight, the day before Mark's birthday, Petra Grundling from NECSA in South Africa replied to my email and said that if I supplied the name of the person I was looking for, she would make enquiries for me. My sixtieth-birthday present for Mark was now complete and in twenty-four hours' time he was in for a very long and emotional evening.

Geri and I invited Mark and Mo to our house because it is impossible to guarantee you will not be interrupted at their home, and this was a story I wanted to unveil slowly and with great care. Mark had waited over fifty years for this information and much of it had been deliberately kept from him. He sensed something was up as soon as they arrived, but we had a stalking horse in the form of a conventional birthday present – a large wooden statue of Tin Tin and Snowy, one of his favourite cartoon characters – which got us through dinner.

Over coffee, although always black tea for Mark, I brought out the suede leather binder and told Mark I had been researching his family history, and had just completed it in time for his birthday. I started with his maternal family tree first because he knew some of it already and it served as a warm-up act before moving onto the

Constantine family tree. Now he was noticeably more alert and even slightly on edge because he realised I must know something about his father that he did not.

I explained that, by obtaining his parents' marriage certificate and using the 1911 census, I had been able to find his grandfather and great-grandparents living in a mining village on the outskirts of Manchester, and we could finally put to rest any possibility that he was related to King Constantine of Greece, a long-standing joke.

I revealed that his great-grandfather had been a cabinet-maker in Little Hulton who had had six children, including Mark's grandfather John Hyde Constantine born in 1904. I added that I had tried to trace the families of all those six children (his great-uncles and aunts) but so far had only found three sisters, grandchildren of his great-uncle Ernest, all living in Australia. Like Mark, they were great-grandchildren of Thomas Henry Constantine but not close relatives.

Next, I pulled out his grandparents' marriage certificate and showed him that they had married on Christmas Eve 1927 and that his father had been born in December 1928. Mark confirmed that his father had been an only child, also that he had been in the RAF when he met Mark's mother and that he was a London police constable when they married in 1950. One of the few photographs that Mark had of his father was one taken outside his grandmother's house, dressed in his RAF uniform and holding Diane's hand.

I asked Mark if his mother had ever mentioned his grandparents to him when he was growing up, and he said the only thing she had ever said about them was that 'they were nice people.' It was time for the first exposé: Mark's mother had never told him that they were alive and living in Manchester at any time during his childhood or teenage years. I told him that his grandfather had died in 1970, when Mark was eighteen, and his grandmother in 1988, when he was thirty-six. He said he had no idea his paternal grandparents were still alive during this period of his life, and we paused for a moment while that news sank in.

The atmosphere in our dining room was becoming quite tense as Mark could see that I had a box beside me that I had not yet

1954 -1959

Mark as a young child, found in his grandmother's box of memories

opened. I carried on with my story and explained that I had checked to see if his father had any living cousins on either his grandfather or grandmother's side of the family, but all the ones I had found were no longer living.

I opened the box and slid a photograph across to him face down with a date handwritten on the back in blue ink: '21st July 1959.' 'Before you turn that over,' I said, 'do you recognise the handwriting?' 'My mother's,' he replied, and then, for the first time ever, he looked at the photo-

graph of himself as a seven-year-old boy in his new school uniform. The look on his face said it all but no words came out, so I slid across a couple more photographs of him as a small child in his grandmother's garden and on a day trip to Bournemouth – again, photographs he had never seen. Still struggling to find some words,

Mark looked across to the box, which clearly contained more photographs. 'My grandmother's...?' 'Your grandmother's collection of photographs,' I replied and then, in case he hadn't quite understood, 'your grandmother Matilda, your father's mother.'

That got his pulse racing and he started looking around nervously as if someone was going to walk into the room. I reassured him that it was just us, and gave him the

1959, LITTLE HULTON, MANCHESTER

Aunty June aged 15 with brother John

wedding photograph of his grandparents and one of his grandfather in his World War Two uniform. After another long pause, Mark asked me where all of these photographs had come from. 'From a lady in Manchester,' I replied, and then passed him the photograph of Aunty June and me in her back garden. 'This is your Aunty June, your father's sister.'

I told Mark the story of how I had found Aunty June from the information on his grandmother's death certificate; how we had got in contact and exchanged information that resulted in June sending me her mother's collection of memories; and that I had flown up to Manchester to meet her and her daughter Bernadette. I also explained that June had been adopted as a baby and so was not registered as a Constantine until her marriage in 1963, when she became June Howarth. That was the name under which she registered her mother's death in 1988.

At this point we took a short tea break while Mark and Mo absorbed everything I had told them thus far. Mark knew there was more to come and that it would inevitably contain much-longed-for information about his father. I related what June had told me: that his father had returned from Kenya suffering from a lung illness when she was about fifteen, and I showed him a photograph of June and John in the garden of the family home in Manchester. I told Mark that John had stayed in Manchester until he was well enough to return to Kenya, and that June had next seen him around 1963 when he came home with Prudence Marston Brogan. June also remembered Eric coming to the family home to ask about the whereabouts of John Constantine so that Mark's mother could file for divorce. This would have been around the time that Mark was

1970, CAPE TOWN, SOUTH AFRICA
Mark's father arriving on the SA Oranje

eleven and still living with his mother and grandmother in Wyke Regis. Mark confirmed he had known nothing of this.

The next set of photographs showed John living in Gloucestershire with his new wife and baby daughters, Joanna and Sarie. This was a very poignant moment as Mark discovered he had two half-sisters, born either side of his other half-sister, Laura. I showed him their birth certificates and his father's occupation as a health physics inspector at the nearby Berkeley nuclear power station. There were more photographs of the baby girls on the beach with their grandparents, and then I came to the next big reveal: the family standing on the dockside at Southampton, six months before Mark's seventeenth birthday. 'Your father bought a one-way ticket to South Africa,' I told Mark, 'and he never came back.'

Mark studied the photograph of his father arriving in Cape Town in January 1969 for some time, understanding this was the moment his father had been lost to him forever. Not even his mother or stepfather knew that John had left the country, nor apparently did the private detective that Mark had hired to find him many years later. More photographs came out of the box, revealing Joanna and Sarie growing up in South Africa, and I related June's account of how John had kept in touch with his family, albeit infrequently, until the last set of photographs, which we had dated to around 1982.

'This is the last photograph,' I said, showing Mark the house on the hill and his teenage sisters with their family dog. After that, June and her mother never heard from him again, and couldn't find him either when they advertised in a South African newspaper asking for information on his whereabouts. 'June said your grandmother died of a broken heart.'

It was gone midnight when I finished the story and had revealed all the photographs from the box of memories, including the 1907 family portrait June had given me. Mark was now officially sixty years old and had been parted from his father for fifty-eight of those years. Only one question remained unanswered, and it didn't need asking. 'Mark, I don't know whether your father is dead or alive, but I know where to find him.'

Mark just nodded: 'Finish it.' He picked up the book of his family history and the box of family photographs. I wrote down Aunty June's telephone number and address, then we all hugged each other and said goodnight. There was nothing left to say; we were all emotionally drained.

The next day I fired off my second email to Petra Grundling at NECSA and went away on a week-long sailing holiday. In the meantime, Mark and Aunty June spoke on the phone, which must have been wonderful for both of them. When I returned the following Saturday I found a reply from Petra waiting in my inbox, but above it was another email from Joanna Constantine. It read:

Dear Jeff,

I am John Constantine's daughter Joanna, and this is wonderful news! Yes my dad is still alive and living with me. I think he will be really happy to hear that you have taken all the trouble to make contact.'

She included her address in South Africa and telephone number. I hadn't mentioned Mark in my emails, as I still did not know to what extent John's daughters knew about his previous marriage and the fact that he had a son. I texted Mark three words: 'Found him alive.'

My job was done and I left it to Aunty June to call Joanna and make contact with her niece and brother. Joanna and Sarie knew their father had been married before and had a son called Mark. They had even tried looking for him on Ancestry.com but searched his stepfather's surname Rogers, which of course had yielded no results. Eighty-three-year-old John Constantine was not in good health and was hard of hearing so he was unable to talk on the phone but, through Jo, Mark asked if he could come and visit him, and his father replied that he would love to meet him.

I found out in a strange way though. I was filming Mark's keynote speech at the September Lush managers' meeting when Mark told me to switch off the cameras and come on stage. He handed me a microphone and asked me to tell his staff the story of how I found his father. No warning, no preparation, just: 'Hello I'm Jeff and I've known Mark since we were in Wolf Cubs together when we were ten years old.'

Mark has always instilled in his staff a sense of kind-heartedness, and they occasionally reward a customer for what Lush calls 'a random act of kindness' with a small gift to make their day. He told the managers' meeting that my birthday present to him, finding his father, was the greatest act of kindness he had ever known and that straight after the meeting he was getting on a plane to Johannesburg with Mo and his children, to finally be reunited with his father. Mark hadn't been able to go earlier as he was filming a documentary for the BBC where he told the presenter, of *Dragons' Den,* Peter Jones, on camera that he had recently come to the conclusion that he had spent his whole life trying to impress a father whom he had never met. He calls it the 'entrepreneur's wound', hidden deep in his psyche, but identified it as the primary source of his drive and determination to succeed.

In late September 2012 I was waiting nervously by my phone knowing that over five thousand miles away Mark and his family were arriving in South Africa where his two half-sisters Joanna and Sarie were waiting to greet them. Having lived with Mark's story for the past nine months during my search, I could only imagine how he must have felt on the drive from Johannesburg to Jo's house and the seconds before walking into the room where his father was waiting for him. Mark's son Jack recalled those moments:

'We pulled up to Aunty Jo's house to be greeted by lots of rescue dogs and cats in a lovely front garden with a beautiful lemon tree in the centre. Walking up to the porch the anticipation was palpable as Dad led the way through the front door, and we followed him into a familiar feeling lounge where John was sat wrapped in a blanket in his wheelchair. Dad headed to the nearest seat next to him and the rest of us scattered across the lounge on sofas and chairs watching with our hearts in our throats as Dad met Grandad for the first time in fifty-eight years.'

Seconds later Mo sent me a text message and a photo of that historic moment. 'John Constantine, I presume,' is what I might have said, but it was 'Hello, Dad, I've really missed you,' to which his father replied: 'You're very confident ... I've missed you too.' John Constantine had immediately tried to apologise to his son but Mark had told him there was no need to, it wasn't a time for regrets or admonishment, they just enjoyed sitting quietly together. John Constantine was a very frail old man and the anticipation of meeting his son, after so long apart, must have been as anxious a time for him as it was for Mark.

After tea, Mark presented his father with a gift box containing a *'Dear John'* bottle of cologne and its accompanying description, written by the creator: 'This was the perfume that gave me the assurance to call myself a perfumer. With a warm citrus splash and strong coffee note Dear John seems strange and familiar at the same time.'

The message in a bottle – an imagined scent of a son burying his face in his father's jacket - was now delivered in person and John Constantine's eyes filled with tears, as he smelt the perfume that bore his name.

John and Joanna had actually moved away from Pelindaba to a small village north of Johannesburg, but one with a lovely garden and lots of African birds for Mark to tick. It turned out that his younger sister Sarie was also an avid birder, and Jo was an animal lover and environmentalist, so there was instant chemistry between Mark and his siblings. Their mother Prudence had passed away some years earlier, and while Jo had remained single, Sarie was married to Stu Mackinnon and had a teenage daughter Kyla, now the niece of Mark and Mo Constantine OBE. Mark and his family spent a few days getting to know his father and sisters, and discovered that his dad had also been involved in amateur dramatics at a town in Kenya where the Royal Kenyan Police had posted him. Jo had pictures of him on stage with the cast, and I surmised that this was the town where John had met the Louis family and Prudence, back in the 1950s.

At the end of the week, Mark said his farewells and his father told him that he *had* kissed him goodbye on the night he left for Kenya in 1954. Mark promised to return early in the New Year and bring me with him. Sadly, he was back sooner than expected. Two months later, in November 2012, John Constantine died at his home in South Africa. Mark and Mo returned for the funeral, where they met Petra Grundling from the NECSA pensioners forum who had put me in touch with Joanna. She confessed that she hadn't been sure about whether or not to reply to my email, but she was so glad that she had played her part in the reunion of Mark and his father.

Mark never did get all the answers about his father's enigmatic life. The miner's son who excelled at grammar school but wanted to join the RAF before the war ended; the London police officer who was assigned to the Royal Protection squad but ended up in the Royal Kenyan Police; the man who gave up his wife and baby son, and disappeared into Africa not once, but twice and finally found his way into the secret world of atomic bombs. During that time he had become an alcoholic, but at the age of sixty he decided to turn his life around, give up alcohol and start his own business, which he ran for the next fifteen years. Mark was now sixty and at a crossroads too, particularly with regard to the future direction and the legacy of his company. After carrying an empty ache for most of his life, the brief time with his father gave him the fire to reinvent both himself and Lush.

After returning from his father's funeral, Mark wrote a five-year business plan for the company, called One Lush, which set out the aims and objectives of the company in all areas of the organisation. He gave me a copy and told me to make a special edition of Lush TV for the 2013 June international conference. I travelled all over

2018, AMSTERDAM
Jack speaking at the The Next Web conference

the world – to Lush Dubai, Lush Japan and Lush Hong Kong. I commissioned films from Lush Russia and other Lush countries, and I interviewed key contributors in all areas of the business. Jack Constantine outlined how Lush Digital would impact the business over the coming years, while Simon Constantine illustrated how the SLush fund would enable Lush to support farmers in developing countries and maintain ethically sustainable supply chains for essential ingredients.

Mark, of course, was the key contributor and for the first time ever he allowed me to film him using his own script on autocue so that he could talk directly to his worldwide staff and link into the many features we had filmed to illustrate the One Lush business plan. The film was produced in seven languages so that every member of staff understood where the company was headed and

what it meant for them, both as
countries and as individuals. Much
of what Mark talked about was hard
to imagine; large shops that could
turn over not £1 million a year in
sales, but £2 million. Three years
down the line, a new 9,500-square
foot flagship shop spanning three
floors in Oxford Street would post
sales of £8.1 million in its first year.
Lush would continue to outperform

2015, OXFORD STREET, LONDON
Claire Constantine, first manager

most high-street brands in the face of austerity in Britain and many
other countries, and end the financial year 2018 with 928 shops in
forty-eight countries and global brand sales of just under £1 billion.

Mark also began the difficult process of ensuring Lush would
never go the way of The Body Shop and be sold to another business or venture capitalists. Lush is not just a chain of shops; it is

2015, OXFORD STREET, LONDON
Opening day

an organisation and a family
of like-minded people, many
of whom have been with the
company for years. Today,
there is a Lush Employee
Benefit Trust, which holds 10
per cent of the shares in the
company. It's envisaged that
over time the EBT shareholding will increase, as and when,
any of the founding share-

holders retire and wish to sell their shares. So the future of Lush
and its employees is now protected and it can continue to carry the
torch of ethical trading in the cosmetics industry – a torch first lit
by Dame Anita Roddick and picked up by Mark Constantine OBE.

Destiny is a road that does not run straight; it just ends at the same place. In November 2013 Mark, Mo, Geri and I travelled to South Africa to go on safari with Jo and Sarie in the Kruger National Park and see 200 African birds in ten days and all the wonderful wildlife that is the essence of Africa. Before that, though, I travelled with my best friend for one important journey, and this time we did turn up the track beyond the bridge over the Crocodile River as we drove up onto the plateau where John Constantine had built his house. There in the place he loved so much, with its panoramic vista, Mark and his sisters scattered their father's ashes and spilt the contents of a bottle of perfume called *'Dear John'* until it was all carried away on the wind. A message in a bottle from a son to his long-lost father, no longer lost but found just in time, on the road to Pelindaba.

2012, DOORNRANDJE, SOUTH AFRICA

'Sawubona' – Hello

# Mark Constantine OBE
# Family Tree

**JOHN CONSTANTINE**

B Dec 1928 Little Hulton, Manchester, England
M Nov 1950 Wyke Regis Weymouth, England
D Nov 2012, Doornrandje, South Africa

**MARK CONSTANTINE**

B July 1952 Kingston, Surrey, England
M June 1973 West Stafford, Dorset, England

**MARGARET JOAN KENYON**

B June 1953 Warwick, England

**DIANE MERRIEL GARDNER**

B Aug 1930 Dorchester Dorset, England

JOHN HYDE CONSTANTINE

(COAL MINER)

B Dec 1904 Tyldesley, Lancashire, England
M Dec 1927 Barton, Manchester, England
D June 1970 Barton, Manchester, England

THOMAS HENRY CONSTANTINE

(CABINET MAKER)

B 1870 StockportCheshire, England
M 1892 Stockport, Cheshire, England
D 1950, Tyldesley, Lancashire, England

MARY ELIZABETH RILEY

B 1873 Stockport, Cheshire, England
D 1908 Stockport Cheshire, England

MATILDA BRIDGE

B Oct 1905 Little Hulton, Manchester, England
D Jan 1988 Salford, Manchester, England

RICHARD BRIDGE (LABOURER COKE WORKS)

B 1874 Little Hulton, Lancashire, England
M 1899 Bolton, Lancashire, England
D 1958 Lancashire, England

MARGARET ANN BUXTON

B 1876 Radcliffe, Lancashire, England
D 1952 Barton, Lancashire, England

FREDERICK GARDNER

(RAILWAY FOREMAN)

B 1852 Preston, Gloucestershire, England
M 1875 Wolstanton, Staffordshire, England
D 1925 Hereford, England

FREDERICK GARDNER

(GROCER)

B Jul 1885 Hereford, England
M March 1911 Manhattan, New York, USA
D Dec 1938 Dorchester, Dorset, England

EMMA CLARA HAWLEY

B 1854 Wolstanton, Staffordshire, England
D 1895 Hereford, England

ARTHUR BARNARD RUDKINS

(STEEL PLATER FOREMAN)

B 1865 West Ham, Essex, England
M 1889 Stepney, London, England
D 1927 Southampton, Hampshire, England

BLANCHE REBECCA RUDKINS

B 1890 West Ham, Essex, England
D Oct 1964 Weymouth, Dorset, England

JESSIE JEMIMA NEWSON

B 1866 Mile End, Middlesex, England
D 1942 Dorchester, Dorset, England

# Acknowledgements

This story could never have been told until I found June Howarth, forever known as Aunty June. June provided me with the lost photographs that unlocked Mark's missing family history and enabled me to discover the whereabouts of John Constantine. I also have to thank Petra Grundling, the secretary of the NESCA Pensioner's Forum for connecting me with John's daughter, Joanna Constantine, who herself was very instrumental in uniting Mark with his father and providing me with a more complete understanding of John's life in South Africa.

As a first time author, I thought long and hard about whether I could turn this family history detective story into a wider biography about Mark's life, and I have to thank my wife Geri for reading my numerous drafts, many times over, and encouraging me all the way to the finish line. In this respect my close friend Suzi Turner from the Open University corrected much of my grammar and punctuation, and Killian Mullarney improved my choice of words with the same keen eye for detail and language that he applies to his bird illustrations. However at this point the book was still too long and in need of professional editing and I'm indebted to Charlotte Atyeo for making the hard cuts and providing the structural advice that helped me produce a far better final draft than I could have managed on my own. Throughout the project I've been greatly encouraged by Matt Fairhall from Lush who has project managed the publication from start to finish, and numerous friends and former colleagues at Lush who have contributed facts and figures and personal memories.

Finally I have to thank Mark and Mo for trusting me to tell an honest account of Mark's life and the story behind the growth of Lush, without any restrictions.

That story is still ongoing, but this one ended on a hill in South Africa, and although I never met him I'd like to pay my respects to the late John Constantine for inspiring me to do something I always wanted to do – to be a detective!

2012, DOORNRANDJE, SOUTH AFRICA

(Left to Right) Jack Constantine, Kyla Mackinnon, Sarie Mackinnon (née Constantine), Simon Constantine, Joanna Constantine, Mark, Mo, Claire Mays (née Constantine), John Constantine

# List of Illustrations

Most of the photographs in this book come from the family archives of Mark Constantine and Jeff Osment, and were taken by themselves, family, friends, and photographers official and unofficial lost in the mists of time.

Photographs relating to Constantine & Weir and Cosmetics To Go have generally been commissioned from professional photographers including:

Jeff Osment / Dave Blunden – CTG Kilimanjaro Expedition / Clive Holmes Studios – Cosmetics To Go catalogue photographs and illustrations

The portrait of Anita Roddick and Mark Constantine p91 was taken by Charlie Stebbings

Endpapers illustrated by Rachel Norden

Photographs relating to Lush have generally been taken by in-house photographers including: Richard Skins / Felicity Millward / Charlotte Brown

Photographs for the Twitch chapter are courtesy of Mark's birding colleagues, The Sound Approach and Arnoud B van den Berg

Mark and Mo OBEs Windsor Castle p219 courtesy Rowena Bird

The Lush Players photograph p220 courtesy of Hannah Dymond

Maps © Open Street Map contributors

Every effort has been made to trace the copyright holders of the images reproduced. We apologise for any unintentional omission and would be pleased to insert the appropriate acknowledgement in any subsequent edition.

# About the Author

Jeff Osment is a retired filmmaker, who has made over 300 films and videos for industry and business in a 40 year career, starting as a projectionist in a London advertising agency in 1972 and finishing as the creator and producer of Lush TV from 2006 until 2014.

He has travelled all over the world on filming assignments and won international awards for his work. In 2015, he took early retirement and started writing.

*Dear John: The Road to Pelindaba* is his first book.